Conversation Skills

Learn How to Improve your Conversational Intelligence and Handle Fierce, Tough or Crucial Social Interactions Like a Pro

ZAC M. CRUZ

CONVERSATION SKILLS

The information provided herein is stated to be truthful and consistent, in that any liability, in terms of inattention or otherwise, by any usage or abuse of any policies, processes, or directions contained within is the solitary and utter responsibility of the recipient reader. Under no circumstances will any legal responsibility or blame be held against the publisher for any reparation, damages, or monetary loss due to the information herein, either directly or indirectly.

The information herein is offered for informational purposes solely, and is universal as so.

The presentation of the information is without contract or any type of guarantee assurance.

The trademarks that are used are without any consent, and the publication of the trademark is without permission or backing by the trademark owner. All trademarks and brands within this book are for clarifying purposes only and are the owned by the owners themselves, not affiliated with this document.

TABLE OF CONTENTS

INTRODUCTION

Have you wondered how different your life would look like if you were both socially confident and a great conversationalist?

A lot of people have a deeply ingrained belief that it is academic ability and intelligence quotient what has the most profound influence on our success in life. But there is substantial evidence now that shows that it is our ability to adapt to our social environment what has more impact on how well we fare in critical areas of our life.

And it's not complicated to see why: humans, by nature, are social animals that have got mainly to where we are now thanks to our enhanced sense of social awareness. It is our ability to cooperate with others on a large scale and our imagination and reasoning that sets us apart from the rest of the animal species.

It can be limiting to think that social and conversation skills are mainly to make new friends. Being skilled at these help us communicate with others, learn more efficiently, ask better questions, make new friends, get better career opportunities, properly close business deals, form stronger connections with others, create a long-lasting impression, develop and maintain relationships, etc. The list of benefits goes on and on.

On the other hand, not having good social skills can have devastating effects and can even end up impacting our physical and mental well-being. We now know that having poor social skills is connected to experiencing feelings of loneliness, depression and other mood disorders. We tend to feel at our best when we connect with others and when we're sharing experiences and emotions. Recently, it has also been found that a lack of social skills can even impact our physical health.

In my case, before I decided to get this area of my life sorted out, I was timid around people, anxious and had low self-esteem. If you had asked friends and family to describe me, none of them would have uttered the words "good conversationalist," "sociable," "assertive" or "confident."

I was deeply aware of this fact, and it just left me feeling more miserable until I finally mustered up the courage to get this and several other related areas of my life handled for good.

Whenever I saw someone speak up their minds, and often get what they wanted, I secretly wished I dared to do the same. I started to question if they had specific personality traits that made it so easy for them to be so vocal about their thoughts. After all, I was an introvert, and introverts are supposed to be shy and quiet, right?

Most tend to believe the false paradigm that people are born a certain way – for instance; you are either charismatic or you aren't. Or you are born a passive guy or gal, or you're an aggressive one. But in reality, there are several attributes that we can develop by consciously modifying our behaviors through constant practice. It took me a while to realize that this is possible. The thought of being an introvert that wasn't shy or afraid of speaking his mind clashed with what others had taught me and what I had experienced throughout my life.

Nowadays, I love interacting and having great conversations with different kinds of people, especially strangers.

It's an exciting thought to think that I can form a connection with another person out of thin air, without knowing anything about him or her beforehand. This has all been possible after dealing with the social anxiety that accompanied me for years and the conversational skills that I developed from almost scratch.

I wrote this guide for those who feel that their social skills, particularly their conversation skills, are lacking and perhaps even affecting their life negatively in specific ways. It doesn't matter if you're starting from pretty much zero (just like I was) or if you're already decent, you'll probably find some useful advice that will help you progress and improve, whether your goal is to make new friends or to be the life of every party you attend.

Thank you, and I hope you enjoy the journey!

CHAPTER 2: DEALING WITH SOCIAL ANXIETY

A lot of people want to become better conversationalists, meet new people, or increase their social intelligence, but there's a significant roadblock that's preventing them from reaching these goals: social anxiety.

Social anxiety has to be addressed first to make any form of progress. If you're continually experiencing negative feelings before, during and after social interactions, then it's going to be extremely hard to focus on specific advice that helps you become better at being a good conversationalist.

In my case, I had almost crippling social anxiety that prevented me from going to most social gatherings and avoided most situations where I had to deal with or face several people that I didn't already know. I was even deathly afraid of going to shows and events, out of the irrational fear of being called out from the audience and not knowing how to react or what to say.

Try to answer the following questions honestly:

-Do you tend to avoid social gatherings such as parties or reunions because you feel self-conscious or nervous while at them?

-Do you avoid certain social situations, even if they might increase your happiness or quality of life because of how shy you are?

-Are you always worried about what others might think of you during social situations?

-Do you feel like what you have to say is of little worth to others?

-Do you dislike being the center of attention out of worry that others might notice how anxious you are?

If you answered yes to one or more of these questions, then yep, you've guessed it: you probably have some degree of social anxiety. Social anxiety is not a black and white thing – you might feel relaxed and at total ease in certain situations, but stressed out and nervous in others.

For some people, social anxiety can be very crippling, and it may even affect their health and impact their quality of life very negatively.

Some of the most common symptoms of social anxiety are: feelings of embarrassment, feeling vulnerable, being too self-conscious, increased perspiration, change of voice tone, dizziness, stuttering, blushing, etc.

The causes of social anxiety

There are several explanations for what may cause social anxiety. There's a substantial amount of research that suggests that past events in our lives can cause social anxiety. For instance, imagine that you inserted your finger in an AC socket when you were little. After getting a mild electrical shock, this event would teach you that AC sockets are dangerous and that inserting your finger in them will cause you harm, so doing this should be avoided. Going back to social anxiety, if you ever went through a social interaction where you felt embarrassed, awkward or uncomfortable during or afterwards, then you will try to avoid that event in the future as a way to protect your feelings.

Imagine a child speaking in front of his classroom, and something terrible happens (such as forgetting what he was going to say or doing something unintentional that made others laugh at him). That child is probably going to be afraid of speaking in front of others the next time, as he will be worried that a similar situation will repeat itself in the future. Because of this, he will start avoiding such cases like the plague, and eventually develop social anxiety.

There's another theory that suggests that people with a particular style of thinking tend to develop social anxiety more easily; people with a pessimistic attitude that are always thinking that they will perform poorly in social interactions are prone to develop social anxiety. Others that believe that people are still paying attention to them and scrutinizing their actions are also more likely to develop social anxiety. Some have developed negative beliefs about themselves in social interactions.

For instance, if someone believes that their opinion is of little worth and that they rarely have something of value to offer in social interactions, this usually translates to higher levels of social anxiety. These negative beliefs are continually working against them.

Interestingly, there are some more theories about other factors that may cause social anxiety. Some experts believe that some people may be more prone to develop social anxiety due to genetics. If someone in their family tends to have social anxiety, there's a higher chance that others in their family will also be socially anxious. It seems to be true that our genes play a part in how likely we are to develop social anxiety.

Human beings are social creatures that tend to thrive when they are constantly interacting with others. Because of this, some social behavior experts believe that social anxiety is connected to the human fear of upsetting or disappointing other members of our society.

Disappointing others might mean that you will be rejected and thus, "abandoned" by your group, and therefore left to survive alone. This fear is deeply ingrained in most people since survival is one of the highest priorities of most us. Those that are socially anxious might be more sensitive than usual to this constant worry of being rejected by their group.

In many cases, it may be a combination of the several reasons mentioned above and not just one that may cause an individual to develop social anxiety.

Why do people have a hard time overcoming their social anxiety?

A lot of people are already aware that they have a problem in social situations, and they still aren't able to do something about it.

Overcoming social anxiety is even harder to those that tend to think negatively, because their unhelpful thoughts make a big dent in their levels of social confidence, making it tougher for them to try and improve their situation. Because they are continually avoiding social situations, they rarely get the chance to see how good or bad their social skills are in practice. Sometimes it only takes one positive experience to help them change their mind. Having a positive experience can begin to disprove negative thoughts and preconceptions, and can be one of our strongest allies when we are trying to change our behaviors. Also, the more that we tend to avoid a social situation that gives us anxiety, the more difficult it will be to face in the future.

There's a point though, found between avoiding a social situation and facing it: using "safety behaviors." Sometimes, those that experience social anxiety decide to face the situation or may have no other choice.

In these cases, they resort to using safety behaviors; safety behaviors are behaviors that help them feel more comfortable in social situations but do nothing to help address the root cause of their social anxiety. For instance, if someone is afraid about going to meetings where their coworkers and their boss is present, but they have no other choice, they might have found out that by remaining quiet, most will ignore them and will rarely have to deal with any challenging or uncomfortable situations. Other coping mechanisms that some people use often are taking drugs to deal with the feelings of anxiety or sitting at the back of a room to remain unnoticed.

For some, it may seem like resorting to these behaviors is the way to go. After all, you manage to go through the social situation, but nothing terrible tends to happen, and you rarely have to face your fears. However, this can be a very damaging strategy in the long run, because it is similar to a band-aid that does little to solve the root of the problem.

By using safety mechanisms to protect yourself from having to deal with your social fears, you will never have the chance to see how you would have coped if you faced the situation head-on. Because of this, your low confidence remains the same, and your beliefs remain rooted in negativity as always. Another con of this strategy is that people might start seeing you as uncooperative or antisocial because of your constant low efforts.

Those that have a pessimistic attitude not only think pessimistically before facing a social interaction but also afterward. It's common for these people to focus only on the negative and convince themselves that they performed worse than they did in reality. For instance, they might have done ok when delivering a public speech in front of others, but they may begin focusing on a specific mistake they did or something an awkward habit of theirs that they think others might have noticed.

Those that tend to suffer from social anxiety are very self-aware of how their body is feeling while they are participating in social interactions. Their focus might be on whether they are stuttering, coming across as weird, blushing, sounding too needy, etc., which causes them a lot of harm in the long run as it is akin to putting more gasoline in a fire. They may think that by focusing on how their body is feeling they will be able to avoid mistakes and embarrass themselves, but in reality, being incredibly self-aware in a negative way can be very detrimental when interacting with others.

As you may already know, charismatic people or those that are socially intelligent tend to be very skilled at remaining present in the moment. Most of their focus is on the person they are talking to and not on themselves. It is this ability that helps the people they interact with feel special and plays a significant role when trying to build rapport and make connections.

If most of your focus is on being worried about the way you are feeling and thinking instead of on the conversation, you won't be able to give reasonable responses and talk fluidly, which will only worsen the negative beliefs you have about your performance in social situations.

Overcoming social anxiety

The good news is that no matter how socially shy we are, in most cases, there's a lot in our hands that we can do to reduce our social anxiety. Let's take a look at some of the most powerful strategies we can use to achieve this.

-Challenging our negative beliefs: If we were able to look inside the mind of charismatic leaders or those that tend to be great conversationalists, we would quickly notice that there are little to no negative thoughts influencing their behaviors.

People that tend to suffer from social anxiety are the opposite: the amount of negative feelings they have hinders their ability to perform well in social interactions. If this is your case, then the first thing to be conscious of is that our thoughts are simply that: no more than thoughts. They are not real, and they rarely have facts to support their "claims."

We can use this as a start to challenge the negative beliefs we have about ourselves since they are more often than not based on wrong assumptions. This technique is called by some cognitive reframing, and it's a staple of cognitive-behavioral therapy. Cognitive Reframing can be a handy tool to help people reduce their stress and anxiety through the implementation of better habits.

To help you with this, let's see some of the most common unhelpful thoughts and negative beliefs that we have before, during, and after a social interaction that might cause you social anxiety.

Before a social interaction you fear, you might be thinking that you will embarrass yourself, have nothing worthwhile to contribute or that there's X physical defect of yours that others might notice and start laughing.

During the social interaction, you might think that people are scrutinizing your every move, that people might notice you're blushing or sweating or that they want you to fail and make a fool of yourself.

After a social interaction is over, you might think that the people you were talking to didn't even pay you attention, thought you were stupid or that you sounded funny.

You might also believe that others think you're uninteresting or weird, but not have any substantial evidence to support this. Over time, this will make a massive dent to your sense of self-worth and self-esteem.

You could also start overgeneralizing. Say if you once had a bad experience while giving a speech in front of others, you might think that any other attempts moving forwards will be similar and end in disaster.

Although these are some of the most common examples of unhelpful thoughts, it's not always easy to identify the ones we deal with regularly. If you're having problems with this, the best thing you can do is to think about a prior social event where you felt anxious. Try then to think about the types of things that might be running through your mind before, during and after that event.

Whenever we start having negative thoughts, they are almost always accompanied by predictable behaviors. For example, before going to a social event, we fear we might begin to try and predict the outcome by spending a lot of time thinking about all the ways that we might embarrass ourselves during the social interaction or all the things that might go wrong.

These predictions rarely become a reality, and, in the end, have put a lot of unnecessary stress and pressure on ourselves.

It may sound difficult at first, but once you recognize any unhelpful thoughts, challenging them is relatively simple. Just like with any other skill, the hardest part is the beginning. However, after some practice, you'll start finding it all more natural and more manageable.

Questions to help you challenge unhelpful thoughts:

Having noticed an unhelpful thought, you can ask yourself – are there any facts that contradict this thought? For instance, imagine that you fear a meeting with your boss because you're afraid that you might say something stupid. Try to think if something like that has happened in the past or not.

You might have coped fine during previous meetings, and you've never said something stupid. Try to think if there was a time that you even did well during a similar social interaction. For instance, you might think about the time where you suggested a good idea to your boss, and both he and your co-workers appreciated your input and nothing negative happened.

See if there are any unhelpful patterns of thinking that you can catch. Using a similar example, you might find yourself trying to predict the future before going to bed or in the morning before such a meeting at work. Be aware whenever you're doing just that, predicting the future without any substantial evidence.

What would an unbiased and honest friend say about the negative thoughts going through your mind? They would probably say that there's no reason why you should be afraid of such meetings since you've never embarrassed yourself in the past or said stupid things.

If you did do something wrong, your friend might help you find the reason why this happened. For instance, you might not have been well-prepared and said something stupid when your boss asked you about something. In this case, you can ensure that this won't happen by taking enough time to prepare yourself enough so that you start feeling more confident before the event.

Ask yourself: how much importance will you give to the social interaction that is causing you anxiety today in the next 3 or 6 months? The reality is that you probably won't even remember it, or it will have no impact on your overall life, and it will be well forgotten by then. Sure, there are some exceptions, as some social interactions can have a significant effect on your quality of life, but this is rarely the case.

How are these thoughts and beliefs affecting your life positively and negatively? Often, those thoughts are adversely affecting your life by making you feel incompetent, nervous and worthless.

On the other hand, these thoughts will have little to no positive effects. You will rarely be able to come up with a benefit.

After answering some of these questions, you'll be able to look at things from a different perspective. For instance, instead of thinking that the meeting will go wrong and that you'll embarrass yourself in front of your boss and coworkers, you can reframe your thoughts and say something like: "I have no facts to support the belief that I'll perform poorly during the meeting and embarrass myself in front of others. This hasn't happened to me during previous meetings, so there's no reason for me to think this way. In fact, there have been a couple of sessions where I've been able to contribute positively, and everyone was appreciative of my input. I have no way of predicting the future, but all evidence points towards the fact that I'll be fine during the meeting and nothing terrible will happen to me."

How to reduce levels of self-awareness during social interactions

As mentioned previously, whenever we are socially anxious, we tend to become negatively self-aware of our actions, and we start focusing too much on how our body feels. We do this primarily because we want to make sure that our nervousness isn't visible to others.

Depending on what you fear, your self-awareness will be heavily influenced by that. For instance, if you're nervous that others might notice that you're sweating, you might always be focusing on whether or not there's sweat on your forehead or hands, completely taking you away from the present moment and preventing you from having a smooth flowing conversation. Others might be worried about their performance during social interactions, so they are always trying to monitor for signs of how well they are doing.

Worry and negative self-awareness also take away from giving proper attention to the social interaction you're having and won't help you make a good connection with someone else or an audience.

When you find yourself becoming negatively self-aware during social interactions, remembering some of the following may be of big help:

-Your nervousness and anxiety are much less noticeable to others than what you think.

-Focus your attention from outside your body and unto the conversation.

-Even if others notice that you are nervous, they won't necessarily think badly about you. Most have been in a similar situation and know how it feels. You are not weird because you're feeling nervous.

-Avoid replaying previous parts of what you've said in your mind, as this will quickly take you away from the present moment and what the other person is saying. At the same time, do not try to be thinking about what you or others will say next, as it will have a similarly negative effect.

-It's not necessary to be perfect. A lot of people feel social anxiety because they fear they might not perform to the high standards that they have set for themselves. Remember that this is unnecessary. You will do fine in most social interactions even if you're not perfect and make a few mistakes here and there.

-Remember the spotlight effect. The spotlight effect is a prevalent cognitive bias that makes us think that we are the center of attention at all times and that people are always looking at us way more than they are in reality. The spotlight effect makes us assume that others are more likely to notice our faults and mistakes.

Because we see things using our perspective first, it can be challenging to imagine how others see you through their lens. In many cases, people won't even notice our mistakes or errors.

-Don't wear a mask. Stop trying to be someone that you aren't when interacting with others. Remember that it's practically impossible to make everyone like you and that you'll come across as a more genuine person by merely trying to act like yourself.

How to face our fears

Socially anxious people tend to avoid social situations that make them feel uneasy. However, this does nothing to help the fact that their sense of self-belief is very harmful and low.

Those that manage to confront their fears and do not avoid social situations resort to the "safety behaviors" mentioned previously that help them cope with the discomfort, but still do nothing to help them in the long run.

So what is the best way to honestly face our fears and diminish the nervousness and anxiety we feel towards them in the long run? Exposure is the key. Gradual exposure to be more specific. There's enough evidence that shows how exposure helps reduce our feelings of anxiety eventually. If you stay in an uncomfortable situation for long enough, your body and mind inevitably start to adapt and feelings of nervousness, stress and anxiety drop.

In some cases, this might even happen in a few minutes. In others, repeated exposure is necessary. In my case, it was constant, repeated exposure to situations that I feared that eliminated my crippling social anxiety for good.

Let's see how to do this in a well structured and non-shocking way:

-Your first step should be to brainstorm for ideas. Think about all of the social situations that tend to put you into a state of discomfort and anxiety. You should include any situations that you tend to avoid and even those that you confront but end up using "safety behaviors" in. For instance: making eye contact with people, talking to strangers, going to a party, talking over the phone, asking for a refund, asking your boss for a raise or days off work.

Once you've come up with a list of situations that cause you social anxiety, try to grade each item with a number from 1 to 100, 1 being zero anxiety and 100 being extremely high, life-affecting levels of anxiety. Once you do this, reorder the items from the situation that you graded the lowest to the highest.

-You should then start taking action. Your first objective should be to confront the first item from your list. The one that gives you the least amount of anxiety, but still gives you some. In my case, I was even afraid of asking a stranger for the time, but I knew that I was able to do it if I mustered up enough courage. While you are exposing yourself to the social situations, it's important to remember the following for best effect:

The more time you expose yourself to such a situation, the more your anxiety and levels of discomfort will diminish. The good news is that in several cases, it will only take you a few minutes or even seconds for most of the anxiety to disappear, but certain situations will require more time. Remember that no matter how difficult it may seem, the anxiety will eventually drop if you stay long enough.

Shoot for trying to reduce the anxiety at least in half.

Say that you wrote "talking over the phone" in your list and that the number "15" is beside it. In this case, you can proceed to the next item in your list when the level of anxiety you feel drops to at least a "7". In some cases, the level of anxiety you feel might even increase while you are performing the task. If that's the case, push yourself to remain in the situation or do the same thing over and over, until the level of anxiety drops by half. Most difficult situations might take up to 30-40 minutes to reach this point, but don't get discouraged if you need more time.

You should avoid resorting to safety behaviors at all cost because they defeat the purpose of this exercise and won't do you any good in the long run.

Whenever you feel discouraged, remember that you are not different or weird for experiencing social anxiety. It's a healthy physiological response that most people feel.

-Your next objective should be to repeat the exposure. If you've managed to reduce the level of anxiety you felt by half when talking over the phone, then try doing it again. Your work is not done yet. You might feel when you reinitiate the activity that your anxiety levels rise, but they typically should be lower each time you engage again in a similar situation. A word of advice: it's essential to do this exercise as often as possible. If you're able to, try to do the exposure task at least once every day until you start feeling more and more at ease with the activity.

-Go to the next item on your list. Once that you manage to feel comfortable, and there are little to no signs of anxiety while performing an exposure task, then you're ready to move to the next item on your list. The cool thing about doing this exercise is that, as you perform the activities more and more, you'll start noticing that some of the items that you had marked with a higher anxiety number will begin to appear less and less scary. This happens because you're starting to develop a greater sense of self-belief and confidence in your abilities.

With enough time and repeated exposure, you'll be able to tackle the item on your list that you marked as being the scariest.

-If you're like me, you might have trouble doing this on your own. What greatly helped me was to enlist a friend (preferably someone you trust, and better yet if he also has some degree of social anxiety) and to make it all a fun game. We would go out each day and challenge ourselves to do stuff that gave us social anxiety. To this day, I still remember this period as some of the most fun I've ever had. Going out every day and pushing ourselves to perform things that we were scared of gave us one of the best natural highs we had experienced, bar none. I later learned that this is how our bodies reward us for massively stepping out of our comfort zones.

You've hopefully found the ideas on this chapter useful to help cure your social anxiety. Remember that these strategies can be used over and over again until you achieve the desired effect.

If you don't notice much of a benefit at first, stick to them for several days or weeks until you start noticing some improvement. It may sometimes take some time to see some noticeable progress, and you'll eventually destroy one more roadblock on your path to becoming a social ninja. The level of freedom and confidence that you'll gain by managing your social anxiety cannot be understated.

CHAPTER 2: THE ROAD TO BECOMING MORE SOCIAL

Most introverts and shy people want to become more sociable. They simply don't know how to start or how to make the first move. Without a game plan or structure, getting better at becoming more sociable isn't something that happens naturally. It can be especially challenging if you're currently suffering from some form of social anxiety or fear of rejection.

To improve your social skills and start making it all a habit, here are a few easy suggestions that you can implement in your daily life right now that will help you get where you want to be in the shortest amount of time possible:

Set goals to help you get there quicker

There is a reason why goal setting is mentioned in pretty much every self-help book out there: it often tends to work. If you're currently not as social as you would want to be, start by asking yourself what exactly you'd like to achieve before you invest your time and energy. For instance, your end destination might be to expand your social circle and meet new friends. Another reason could be to have more options when dating. Or you might want to become better at networking so that you can always have better connections to help boost your career or business. Whatever the bigger picture might be, it's good to be aware of it and keep it in mind. Merely wishing to become more sociable won't help you at all.

Once you've done this, it's time to set up smaller goals that will help carry you there. For instance, if your bigger picture goal is to make new friends and expand your social circle, then you can start by trying to make small talk with at least one stranger every day.

Or you could try assisting events that you're interested at least once per week so that you find like-minded people. Don't be afraid to start small to build up your courage. Once you get going, it's best to keep the momentum going.

Take the first step

Introverts and shy people tend to be afraid to take the first step in social situations. In parties or gatherings, they are rarely the ones that approach others. It's not necessary to wait for other people to take the first step. If you always adopt this frame, then you won't be able to advance your social skills quickly at all.

Instead, try being the one that takes the first step. It is an excellent practice to build up your social confidence and courage. If you wish to go out with your friends, but no one is suggesting anything then pick up the phone or message someone and set something up.

In many cases, people tend not to be social enough not because they were born shy, but because they are too lazy to get into the habit of taking action and making the first contact.

Make it all about them

You'll quickly stand out from the rest if you become good at listening and asking questions. Most people engaged in conversations aren't listening, but merely waiting for their turn to speak or they're trying to be the loudest individual in the room.

At our core, we are all a bit egocentric, and quickly feel connected to people that are interested in hearing our stories. People that seem interested in what we have to say look interesting to us! It's funny how that works. Remember that it's always about them and not you. Being conscious of this fact makes it easier for you since you aren't the one that has to do the talking most of the time.

Asking questions is a great way to keep others engaged because when you ask something to your conversation partner, they feel obligated to answer. To avoid sounding like a questions robot though, you can use the following safety net: question-listen-statement-question-repeat

For instance:

Person 1: (makes a question) I heard that you went to the classical piano concert last night, how was it?

Person 2: Oh, it was great! Some of the best pianists in the country played, and I heard some of my favorite songs.

Person 1: (makes a statement, then asks a question) Sounds like you had a blast.

I've been wanting to go to a classical guitar concert myself, but haven't been able to find a good venue that's not too far away from where I live. In which theatre was yesterday' concert?

And so, on.

Being curious about others makes you more interesting in their eyes. Whenever you're talking to someone, and you'd like to make a good impression on then, find out what motivates them, what they like to talk about, what's most important to them and what they value the most in life. If you're able to answer all of these questions after talking to someone, you can almost guarantee that they'll think of you in very favorable terms. The person will find you so fascinating that they will be looking forward to your next encounter.

It's possible to become good at conversation by knowing how to ask good questions.

In sales, one of the first things taught is that the person that's asking questions tends to be the one in control. So, if you want to know more about someone, and be seen as more likable at the same time, don't be afraid to ask questions.

Never start on a low

A lot of people aren't aware of how the first things you say in an interaction have a powerful effect on the remainder of the conversation and at how others perceive you. For instance, if soon after you greet a stranger you tell them about the awful discussion with your boss you had yesterday, then they will quickly categorize you as being the type of person that tends to complain a lot, is pessimistic or isn't fun to be around.

What you say at the beginning of the interaction tends to set the tone for the rest of the conversation.

If you want to make friends easily and be seen as more charismatic, likable or social, remember always to try and start with a high instead of a low.

For instance, say that you're talking to someone new at work. Try to mention something positive about the current day or the previous day. "Good morning. We had great weather yesterday and looks like it will continue today. I hope that it remains like this for the rest of the week!"

That statement would have a much more positive response than something like "Good morning. I bet that this sunny weather won't last for more than a day. I'm so tired of the rain in this city".

Be open-minded

People that tend to have a hard time making new friends or have a tiny circle of friends not by choice are often narrow-minded. To be able to make new friends without much difficulty, it's essential to try and keep an open mind so that you mix in with others. There is no question that first impressions are crucial and very difficult to shake off afterward, but you'll never know about a person's real personality if you're not able to see past the initial layer.

For instance, someone that dresses in expensive clothing and drives luxury cars might not necessarily be rich. They could be in debt just to be able to look rich.

Once you get to know about someone's personality and interests, you can make a better decision whether you'd like to become friends with them or not.

If there's something about their character that you don't really like, then there's no need for you to hang around them the next time. There's a lot of people that will fit in your idea of a friend. Because of this, try to keep an open mind and don't lock yourself up.

Say yes more often

A big part of improving your social life involves saying yes more often to plans, even if they might not sound ideal at first. In the past three months, how many times have you declined invitations from your friends or colleagues to participate in activities such as parties, dinners, friendly meetings, hiking, watching a movie, etc?

Saying yes to invitations can be more difficult to introverts than extroverts. For an introvert, spending the evening at home watching a movie or reading a book is often more appealing than stepping outside and interacting with others in a social environment.

However, if you start saying yes to a lot of activities, you'll probably be surprised at just how much you enjoy some of them. Another side benefit of saying yes more frequently is that you'll start receiving more invitations for social activities since people know that you tend to say yes.

Expect to make mistakes

Whenever we're learning a new skill, it's inevitable to make a lot of errors, especially in the early stages. It might feel disappointing to some people to hear that even with a guide or a teacher, making mistakes is inevitable. The reality is that, save for some rare cases with people who are naturally gifted at certain things, it's expected to be awful at something before becoming good at it.

While it is true that lots of people, especially extroverts that thrive in social environments, tend to "naturally" become good at conversation, most introverts and people that don't consider themselves very social will have to work at it and make lots of mistakes before they genuinely feel comfortable in social settings.

Perhaps you'll feel very awkward and uncomfortable the first times you attempt to make small talk with people you wouldn't usually talk to. And they will probably feel awkward too. There is no way to avoid this. But you can always ask yourself afterward what made you feel that way and then try to improve little by little so that next time it goes slightly better. Be aware that it's inevitable for your ego to suffer a few blows during this process.

Expect yourself to make lots of mistakes in the beginning stages and don't beat yourself up, because you're almost guaranteed to make them. If you're putting in the work, it's a good idea to realize that you're doing the best you could do with your time and knowledge.

CHAPTER 3: BREAKING THE ICE AND MAKING SMALL TALK

Only the most adept social ninjas don't feel a twinge of anxiety when talking to a stranger. Whether it is someone sitting right next to you during a dinner party or someone standing close to you at an event, the fear of chatting with someone you don't know can cause a lot of discomforts and can also be downright paralyzing to those with extreme social anxiety.

However, small talk is an integral part of our success, whether we like it or not. Whether it is getting new clients, speaking with a potential employer, networking, or making new friends, you must be able to know how to build rapport through light conversation.

The first few times, I went out to social events primarily to improve my social skills I was in for a rude awakening: going over to a person and saying the first few words were extremely challenging. I ended up not doing anything and going back home, feeling very defeated.

I later learned that a great way to avoid the problem of feeling paralyzed because of not knowing what to say at first is to have a few topics up your sleeve to help you get the ball rolling.

Some great topics to initiate a conversation with are:

-**The place you're located.** Discussing your surroundings can be an effortless way to break the ice between two strangers. If you're in a noteworthy area, town or venue, then that's your ticket for starting a great conversation.

You can comment on your surroundings or even ask for more information about the place where you're located. If you notice something unusual or eye-catching nearby, then you can also use that to help you initiate a conversation.

Examples:

-Do you know how many stories tall is this building?

-That bakery smells so good. Have you ever gone there?

-I love this theatre. Would you know how old it is?

-Food. Pretty much everyone loves food, and because of this, it can be one of the best conversation starters.

You can always ask someone for recommendations to eat and what you should order.

If they don't usually eat out, you can ask what they tend to eat at home.

Examples:

-I've been trying to find a nice place to eat seafood, would you know about somewhere that's not too far from this area?

-I'm responsible for bringing snacks at a party today for over 20 people. Most of them don't eat meat. May I ask what you would suggest bringing?

Work. Using work as a conversation starter or topic for small talk is almost a cliché. Talking about this topic can sometimes be tricky because the conversation can quickly become a comparison of what you and the other person do for a living.

On the other hand, it can be effortless to begin a conversation with this topic, since pretty much everyone has something to say about it.

Avoid using the same "hairdresser" questions that pretty much everyone uses when they talk about work with others, such as:

-"What do you do for a living?"

-"Where are you working?"

-"Do you like what you do?"

-"How long have you been working there?"

Instead, try to use unexpected and exciting questions. Here are a few examples of these:

-"Oh, so you work in [X Field]? What is your favorite part of your job? OR My friend wants to work in the same field. Do you have any suggestions or advice I should tell him? OR Why did you decide to work in that field?

-"A lot of friends and colleagues have told me [X thing] about that job. What has your experience been like?"

-"What's the most unexpected thing that you weren't able to anticipate about the role you're in"?

-Weather. Just as with work, talking about the weather is one of those ultimate "hairdresser topics." It's definitively not the most exciting conversation starter, but with some creativity, it can be used very effectively to spark some engaging conversations.

For instance, if it's raining, you can ask people what their plans are for the day. Will they stay at home and read a book or watch a movie or do something else? If it's very sunny, you can ask them if they are going to do something outdoors-related.

You can also ask them what their ideal climate is and the reasons why. This question is excellent because it leads the way to other more interesting conversations. You can learn a lot about their personality and preferences by starting with this.

You can also use the seasons similarly. You can ask them what their favorite things to do are during the summer or winter or what are their favorite places during the current season.

Having meaningful conversations

When people think about small talk, the last thing that comes in their minds is a meaningful conversation. But it's not that difficult to steer a conversation towards more profound and more meaningful topics. Here are a few ideas on how to do this effectively:

-Instead of asking lots of "what" questions, use more "why" questions. Whenever you ask a "what" question, you will usually get a simple, direct answer that rarely leads to more exciting things. However, when you ask a "why" question, you start to understand the person's underlying motives, and there are lots of room to explore that can open more conversational opportunities later. For instance, instead of asking "What did you do when you went to San Francisco during the summer," you can ask "Why did you choose to go to San Francisco during summertime?".

-Keep in mind the 20-second rule. The more you talk, especially about yourself, the more the listener gets bored. If you start talking too much about things that are mainly of your interest, the listener might even think that you're a bit self-centered or too chatty. To avoid this, imagine that every time you talk, you have a green light that turns yellow after the first 20 seconds. Once you reach 40 seconds the light turns red, and you risk putting in danger the conversation. The 20-second rule is not strict since there will be times when it's ok to continue talking after 40 seconds, but the majority of the time, it does apply.

-Don't be shy to ask for advice. We all find it very flattering when someone comes to us for advice. Asking someone for advice is a great way to build rapport quickly. People love it when someone asks to share their knowledge and experiences. Asking for advice makes people talk about themselves, which in turn makes them feel good. It's a very helpful tool to have up your sleeve for speeding up rapport!

Ending a conversation

If you've had a great conversation but it's time for you to go and do something else, or you pick up through the other person's body language that they want to leave, then it's good to know how to exit appropriately.

There can be many different reasons to end a conversation. If you notice that the conversation has stalled and is going nowhere, you didn't like the person you're talking to or need to do something else; there are non-awkward ways to exit.

It's essential to have an understanding of how long you can be talking to someone. For instance:

-If you start a conversation with someone while they are busy doing some errands, then unless the conversation is critical to both of you, they will probably want to go back to what they're doing very fast, usually after two or three minutes.

-If you engage in small talk with a co-worker or employee at work, then they will probably want to get back to work after 5-8 minutes.

-If you are calling someone to set up an activity, then it's best to end the conversation quickly and assume they have something to do, so try not to last more than 5 minutes. You'll have more time to talk to them when you meet.

-If you are talking to someone at a friendly gathering or a party where it's expected for everyone to speak with different people and not stay all the night talking to a single individual, then try not to take more than 5-10 minutes with them, unless you hit it off well and things are flowing great.

-If you end up sitting with someone on the bus, a train or a plane, then they might want to get back to reading, listening to music, etc. Of course, this isn't always the case, and they might want to continue talking with you during the trip, so it's wise to look at what their non-verbals are telling you. Do they seem eager to go back to what they were doing? Or do they look like they couldn't care less about it and would instead continue talking with you?

-Your relationship with the other person influences the

way that you can end the conversation while still sounding polite or avoid any awkwardness.

For instance, if you've known the person for a long time, a simple "I've got to go now. Talk to you later" works in most of these cases.

-If you want to exit a conversation with someone that you've just met in a social setting, then something like "It was nice meeting you" will be enough. If you had a great time talking with this person, you might want to exchange contact details.

-If you've met someone at a business meeting or networking event, then a card exchange works great. If there is a business opportunity, then talking about a follow up with them is crucial.

There is nothing wrong with ending a conversation quickly. A lot of people feel like there's some obligation to have a big polite goodbye every time after they talk with someone.

Most of the time, this isn't necessary, and it is possible to end the conversation very quickly without hurting anyone's feelings. Dragging the conversation, on the other hand, is what can make things more awkward.

The following quick and effective lines work well in most situations:

-"I've got to go now. It was great talking/catching up with you."

-"I need to go now. I'll talk to you later."

If the person you're talking to was in the middle of some errand you could say:

-"It was great seeing you. I'll let you get back to do [X thing]".

-"Let's talk later. I'll let you get back to [X thing].

You can also make up something that fits the situation to support the conversation's end. For instance, if it is very late, you can say, "Let's talk later. I'll let you relax and go to bed now".

If you're the one that needs to do something or get back to an errand, then you can say:

-"It was great catching up with you. I've gotta go back to [X errand]"

-"Sorry I can't stay longer, I need to go back to [X errand]

Non-verbal communication

You can also use your nonverbal communication to support your intention. For instance, if you start adjusting your body slightly towards the door/exit or away from the person, then they will, in most cases understand that you need to leave soon. If you're sitting down and then you stand up, then that's another way you can signal that you need to be leaving soon. Glancing at whatever you need to go back to (such as your laptop) can also be helpful.

Leaving a group conversation

In most parties or social gatherings where you've just joined a group of people that are simply standing around and talking, it's not always necessary to say a formal goodbye before leaving. In some cases, when the event is very informal, you can leave if you want to and go to a different group.

Making a simple gesture that indicates that you're leaving is better than simply walking away though. You can make a similar gesture in other settings such as at work, where there's a bunch of people gathered, but you need to go back to your desk.

When the environment is more formal, or you're with a group of people that you've known for a while such as your family, you need to use your judgment. For instance, some groups or families expect you to say goodbye to each member individually. In other groups, just a single farewell addressed to the whole group will be enough.

CHAPTER 4: HOW TO HAVE DEEP CONVERSATIONS

After a while, breaking the ice and making small talk with even strangers will start to feel like second nature. You will know how to find great topics to spark a basic conversation with people you've never met, and you will even start to make new friends and acquaintances because of this.

Most people love to have deep conversations. Personally, one of my favorite things to do is to be sitting with friends talking about topics we all find enjoyable so that we can all have a stimulating conversation.

So, what exactly is an in-depth conversation?

The answer will vary depending on who you ask. Some people will say that a deep conversation is a conversation that is not necessarily of vast intellect, but one that feels very gratifying for everyone involved. Because of this, an in-depth conversation can be intellectual, emotional or just enjoyable. It has to stimulate the participants in a way that small-talk isn't capable of.

Have you ever been talking to someone and you completely lose interest in your surroundings, because your entire focus is on the words coming out of the other person's mouth? We could say that this is a good sign that you've officially moved into deep conversation territory.

So how exactly do you get in a deep conversation in the first place?

The importance of the environment

While it is true that the environment you're in becomes of little importance once you are in deep conversation territory, some places lend themselves better to this type of conversation that others.

For instance, it is not usual for people to have deep conversations while in noisy or high energy places or while in big groups. In-depth discussions can happen in such places, but it is much more difficult; instead, whenever you want to have deep conversations, it is best to choose relaxed and quiet environments.

A precursor of deep conversations is comfort, and the participants need to feel comfortable to get in the right mood. A friend's house or a spot that you and others enjoy regularly going to that is comfortable and quiet are great choices.

Take your time

Think about all the times you've had a stimulating conversation. It is very likely that most of those times, you didn't get into deep conversation territory immediately after you started talking. Getting "in the zone" takes a while, mostly because the participants need to feel comfortable and relaxed first.

This varies depending on you and the people you are talking to but usually takes at least 15 minutes. Don't get stressed out if you notice that you haven't got past small talk topics and it has taken a while. Others will quickly sense when you're trying to force things, and this can very quickly kill the mood.

Getting in-depth

There will be a point in the conversation where all participants feel relaxed and comfortable, and it will be effortless for someone to bring up a deep conversation topic. This topic can be directly related to whatever you're talking about, or it can be loosely related to it.

How to come up with interesting conversational topics

If you are struggling with coming up with interesting topics that make way for deep conversations, you can try doing the following exercise:

During the day, you probably have lots of random thoughts, some of which may come up at random times during the day, such as right before you go to sleep, while you're on the bus, etc.

This is very normal, as most of us wonder throughout the day about things that fascinate us or spark our curiosity.

Whenever we're talking to someone, we rarely bring up even a small fraction of these random thoughts that we have during the day. It's a good idea to document these thoughts by writing them down in a notebook, app, or by using voice memos.

The next time you start to notice that you are getting into deep conversation territory (when everyone is comfortable and relaxed, and topics are flowing smoothly), you can refer to your list of notes and choose a topic that is loosely related to what is currently being talked about.

Asking personal questions

Asking personal questions is a great way to help things get into deep conversation territory. For instance, if you notice that the conversation has been stuck in small-talk territory for a while, you can try asking something personal.

For instance, imagine that you are talking about how expensive it is to live in your area, and how renting a tiny apartment can be very costly. You can then try asking one of the conversation participants: "So, if money wasn't an issue, where would you choose to live."

Or imagine that the conversation has steered towards talking about work. You can then ask something like: "What would you do if you were to start your own business"?

Asking personal questions early on when the mood is beginning to feel comfortable also makes it more natural for you and others to ask more personal questions later on.

Personal questions can also help add fuel to the fire if the conversation is already in deep territory, as they tend to help people open up more and share more about their thoughts, experiences, and opinions.

Asking open-ended questions is much better than close-ended ones if you want to get in deep conversation. For instance, instead of asking: "Do you like your job?" you could try asking "How does working for X company make you feel?"

A little conversation hack is to ask about people's underlying motivations. For instance, if someone told you that they recently went to India for vacation, you could ask them what made them choose India.

This helps create a window for the other person to share more intimate or in-depth thoughts and experiences. Whenever you ask about someone's underlying motivations, the golden rule is to keep it positive, because it may sound as though you're questioning their choices.

Controversial topics

A lot of people enjoy talking about controversial topics. If you'd like to bring up a controversial topic, avoid bringing it up too early in the conversation. If you're still at the small talk phase, bringing up something controversial so soon might put off others. It's better to bring these topics up whenever everyone is feeling comfortable, and they flow better if they are related to what's being said.

Of course, when you know the people you're talking with very well, you don't have to be as strict as to when to bring up these topics, but it's still a good idea to bring them up once the conversation has some momentum.

If you are dealing with people that might find controversial topics offensive, you can try talking from a third-person perspective to prevent them from getting defensive. For instance: "I've heard that some argue that pain of death should be legal in this country."

Sharing about yourself

It's crucial not to make the mistake of asking deep or personal questions and then avoiding sharing about yourself. This can make others think negatively about you or may make them feel interrogated.

Just remember not to cut others short whenever they're talking to share your experience. Let them speak for a long time if necessary. Whenever they've paused, feel free to share if you have something interesting or meaningful to say. Try to mirror the amount that others have opened up to make everyone feel comfortable. If someone has told an intimate story about a particular topic, then it is ok for you to share a similar intimate story.

It is ok to answer the personal question you've asked others, once it is your turn to speak up. They will most likely find interesting what you have to say about the subject.

Sharing and showing vulnerability, even if it is a small share, will significantly help others open up and feel more comfortable. If you notice that others haven't got to that point yet, don't be afraid of saying something that is slightly vulnerable to make the mood feel more relaxed.

Common conversation obstacles

It's pretty rare to be involved in an engaging, candid, and productive conversation. There are some critical reasons why this happens. We have explored some of them already, but here are others that are worth mentioning

Holding back

In every group of people, there will be those that don't feel very comfortable expressing themselves. You might even still be in this position. Some that are shy or fear getting hurt might want to hold back and not participate enough in the dialogue. However, in all engaging conversations, there tends to be a certain amount of self-exposure involved.

The best way to "break the ice" in this situation is to ask each participant to say a personal experience from their past that relates to the topic discussed. It helps if you can attempt to do this first and act as an example before asking others. Doing this simple exercise helps everyone feel more comfortable with opening up and encourages people to participate more once they've shared their first experience.

Pushed buttons

We all have our weaknesses and weak spots. It's common for us to become defensive whenever someone pushes our buttons, and it becomes tough to have a meaningful conversation afterward.

The solution, as briefly discussed before, is to know what your vulnerable spots are so that you can be in better control whenever someone pushes your buttons, whether inadvertently or not.

Maybe your weak spot is tied to your financial situation or your job situation. Or it could be something more personal. Whatever it is, it's essential to take the time to learn what pokes you.

The participants have different levels of understanding.

It's very common for participants to have different levels of understanding of the topic. Some might be experts in it, while others are just recently learning about it.

To solve this common issue, if you're the one that is most familiar with the topic, then invest some time so that everyone involved in the dialogue is on the same page. On the other hand, if you're the one that is not very acquainted with the topic, then ask the other party to brief you.

CHAPTER 5: THE IMPORTANCE OF NON-VERBAL COMMUNICATION

As you are fully aware by now, our ability to communicate well with others has a significant impact on the success we have in several areas of our life. However, it is not the actual words that come out of our mouths that have the most impact, but our non-verbal gestures and cues that speak the loudest for us.

If our nonverbals aren't aligned with our words to support them correctly, we will be wasting most, if not all of our efforts. Because of this, it is crucial to adequately address this area before moving on to the next chapters.

Three main elements comprise communication:

-Words (what's being said)

-Voice tone (the way the words are being said)

-Body language (conscious or unconscious gestures and movements that help express the information)

There has been a lot of research done to understand better just how important non-verbal communication is when compared to the other two elements, words and voice tone. Some researchers have mentioned that non-verbal communication makes around 90 percent of our total communication.

However, others put this percentage lower, at 50 or 60 percent. While researchers have had a hard time agreeing about the exact percentage, pretty much all of them emphasize non-verbal communication as being the most crucial element out of the three main elements of communication.

There is no doubt that the way you hold eye contact, your facial expressions, voice tone, and gestures are your most powerful communication tool. Having a good grasp on your non-verbal communication will help you build trust and friendship, put others at ease, and help you become more influential or charismatic. On the other hand, not having good awareness and control of your body language (if it's not already good) will cause all kinds of adverse effects when you try to communicate with others, as it can confuse others, hinder your success and undermine the message that you're trying to get across.

By working on your nonverbal communication and improving the way you use it, you will become better at expressing your ideas, opinions, forge stronger relationships and become highly proficient at connecting with others at a deep level.

Understanding body language

Before we start working on our body language, we must first have a good grasp of what it is and what it isn't.

Body language is typically instinctive. Whenever people use body language, they rarely think about it consciously. Most of our physical behavior, which includes gestures and expressions that you've used when communicating with others throughout your life, has mostly been an unconscious effort.

Even if you try to become aware of your body language, there will be certain gestures and micro-expressions that you won't ever know you're doing that will give wordless signals to others. Fortunately, we can dramatically improve a lot of our non-verbal communication with practice.

With nonverbal communication, you don't stop expressing yourself when words stop coming out of your mouth. Even when you remain silent, your facial expressions, postures, and gestures will all be sending signals.

Because of this, a lot of times, the words that come out of our mouths and our nonverbal communication tend to clash with each other. For instance, if you are trying to say with your words that you enjoy someone's company, but your body language is suggesting something very different, your listener will probably figure out that you're dishonest.

An extreme example of how body language and words can clash together is saying the word "yes" to someone while you shake your head (signaling "no"). When doing something like this, your listener will have to choose between one of the two and will often be confused and won't know how to respond correctly. In most cases, however, people will want to follow the nonverbal messages, so it's essential to make sure that our body language supports the words we're saying and doesn't clash with them.

The way we react, the way we listen and move, all send signals to the others. Your listener will receive these signals and often get a good idea of whether you care about what they have to say, whether you're honest or dishonest, and about how well you are listening to them. When your verbal and nonverbal communications are aligned and working together, your message becomes much more powerful, and your words will have a more significant impact, while your ability to increase trust and rapport with others will also increase.

An excellent communicator is profoundly aware and sensitive about his body language and knows how to use it to his favor. Good communicators are also adept at reading the non-verbal communication of others.

Different types of non-verbal communication.

There are several different types of non-verbal communication. Let's take a look at the most important, that will have the most impact on how others see you:

-Posture: The way you sit or stand dramatically affects how others perceive you. Picture someone slouched at their desk at work. Anyone seeing them will probably think that they're tired or bored. Now picture someone that is standing up straight and tall, with their shoulders back; they now seem to appear more engaged and confident.

Connected to your posture is your body movement, as it is complicated to separate these two. The subtle changes you do with your body will also signal several messages to the people you interact with.

-**Facial expressions:** Our facial expressions are a wealth of information to others. After all, what we tend to focus on whenever we speak with someone is their faces, since that's where their mouth and eyes are located. Interestingly enough, out of all the different types of body language, facial expressions tend to be the most instinctive and universal. Whenever we feel, sadness, anger, happiness, or any other emotion, our faces will be one of the first parts of our bodies to reflect what we're going through without consciously thinking about it. Facial expressions tend to be universal and not vary much from culture to culture because of this.

-**Eye contact:** Eye contact is another important element of nonverbal communication.

As is the case with facial gestures, we tend to be looking at someone's face when we're communicating, which is why it is especially important to understand. How you choose to look at someone will signal several things. Your eyes can be powerful tools to convey interest, attraction, anger, nervousness, etc.

If you wish to maintain excellent conversation flow, then learning to read eye contact will be a powerful tool to help you gauge the other person's level of interest.

-**Gestures**: We are continually using gestures every day, and similarly to facial expressions, these are mostly automatic too. For instance, whenever we are trying to make a point, we may use our hands to emphasize a point or to strengthen the power of our words. However, unlike facial expressions, gestures tend to vary a lot from culture to culture. A hand gesture may convey a positive message in western countries but have negative connotations or even be offensive in other cultures.

For instance, in a lot of cultures, the "thumbs up" sign signals approval, but in Bangladesh it is often used as an insult. Other gestures might be so offensive in certain cultures, that they could potentially get you in trouble. For example, the "come here" sign is commonly used in most western countries to ask someone to step forward, but in many Asian countries, it is insulting to use such gesture. This gesture is mostly reserved for calling dogs, and when you use it on a person you are implying they are inferior.

-**Physical contact:** Physical contact or touch is not one of the most often discussed forms of non-verbal communication. However, it is possible to communicate a wealth of emotions through touch. Have you ever heard about how important it is to have a good handshake? Having a weak handshake will immediately signal that you're not entirely confident or comfortable in the situation.

Using other examples, if you're trying to build rapport, a quick and soft touch on the shoulder or arm will help you make a connection quicker. A warm hug will sometimes have a similar effect. On the other hand, using a very firm grip on the same area will signal that you're being controlling.

-**Proximity and space:** You will rarely hear these being mentioned; however, they are still crucial to understand for anyone that wants to improve their communication skills how it influences their interactions. You can probably think about a time where you felt uncomfortable in the presence of others because they were standing too close to you. You probably thought that they were invading your personal space. Even though humans are social beings, we all require our own space. This space can significantly vary depending on our upbringing, culture, level of comfort and trust towards the other person, etc. For instance, if you're trying to signal that you've got better things to do and want to leave the conversation, you might start to move away from the person you're talking with.

Space can also be used to signal affection or attraction. Being close to someone you care about or are attracted to means that you feel comfortable in their presence and have no issue with them being in your personal space.

-**Voice tone:** Have you ever head that the way you say something is much more important than the actual words coming out of your mouth? Well, it is true. Whenever you communicate verbally with others, people are not only paying attention to your words, but they are also reading and interpreting the tone of voice you're using. Sarcasm is one of the best examples of how voice tone can completely alter the final message of your words.

How realistic is it to improve our non-verbal communication?

Some people believe that it's impossible to make dramatic changes to our body language.

Go inside a library or bookstore, and you'll probably find several books that advise how to improve your body language so that you can use it to your advantage.

At the end of the day, if you are genuinely not confident or feel anxious when you're communicating with others, your sub-communications and micro expressions (these are very difficult to control consciously) will reflect how we truly feel. For instance, you might have terrible social anxiety, but you read a book on how to appear more confident when talking with others. You are told to keep a straight back, sit a certain way or shake hands confidently to appear confident and in charge of the situation. What will probably happen is that at some point, your sub-communications and microexpressions will "betray" you and signal to others that you don't truly feel confident.

Because of the above, unless we genuinely feel in charge, our non-verbal communication will not be 100% congruent with what we say.

Unfortunately, whenever we communicate with others, we are sending lots of different signals about how we genuinely feel about the situation, and we can't control all of them. Trying to micromanage most of your communication will be counterproductive, as you will probably be more focused on your body language instead of what the other person is trying to say, which is a recipe for disaster if you're trying to come across as charismatic, friendly, or an excellent communicator.

The great news is that we can take a "fake it until you make it" approach with body language. At first, it might feel like we are putting up a fake persona, and your words and non-verbals will sometimes clash with each other. Over time, as you start receiving more positive feedback and responses when you communicate with others, your social confidence will inevitably improve, and because of this, both your sub communications and microexpressions will start to become more and more aligned to the messages you're trying to convey.

Because you have experience dealing with social situations in the past, you can then draw genuine confidence from those successes. You will no longer feel that you're merely trying to appear as more confident, but instead, you 'll truly feel like you are more confident, friendly, and in control of the situation. Because of all the practice you've done, micromanaging your non-verbals will no longer become an issue. Keeping good posture, maintaining good eye contact and a proper voice tone will all become second nature to you.

Incorrect use of body language

As you know, our non-verbal communication has profound importance as it has a massive impact on how others see us, how much they respect and trust us and also how connected they feel to us. Unfortunately, it is very easy to misuse non-verbal communication, and those that have a high degree of social anxiety or don't haven't developed their social intelligence and calibration tend to suffer the most.

If you've ever thought that someone was socially awkward, their body language probably played a huge role when you drew that conclusion.

Let's take a look at a few examples that we might encounter in our daily lives of how non-verbal communication can be easily misused and the effects this can cause:

-Example 1. Say that you are at work, and there's a new employee that has recently joined your company. His name is Pete, and you are eager to meet him for the first time. However, two of your colleagues that have already met him tell you that Pete is very intimidating and awkward. When you finally get the chance to meet him, you finally understand why. When Pete looks at you, his gaze is very intense, to a point where it makes you feel uncomfortable. When he shook your hand, he did it a bit too firmly, and you got the impression that he isn't there to make any friends and perhaps even sees you as competition.

In reality, Pete wanted to make new friends at the office, but his non-verbal communication is greatly hindering his ability to make any meaningful connections. If he relaxed his gaze more and improved his handshake, people would start seeing him as a much nicer guy instead.

-Example 2. Jim is a single, attractive guy, that seems to have a lot of difficulties maintaining a relationship for more than a few months. He usually has no problem meeting new people, but keeping someone's interest for long is what causes him problems. Even though Jim is interesting and attractive, whenever you speak to him, you can tell that he's feeling a bit anxious, because he's continuously signaling tension. If you take a look at his eyebrows, they are always raised, his voice tends to be high pitched, and his gestures and posture look very stiff. Whenever someone is around him, they quickly begin to feel very uncomfortable. Too bad because Jim has a lot going on for him!

-Example 2. Jackie has just started her new job and is hoping that she can meet new people and make friends. She has always had difficulty making and maintaining friendships though. Even though she is a very interesting and funny person, with many great stories to tell, her body language screams indifference and boredom. When you talk to Jackie, she seems to be looking at anything but you. She also responds with a tone that sounds very unenthusiastic. Anyone that talks to her quickly feel like they're boring her and that she only cares about talking about herself. Jackie actually cares about what others have to say and would love to make new friends, but her body language doesn't do her any favors.

In all of these three examples, the person's real intention is very different from what their body language is signaling.

To avoid any misunderstandings and confusing others when you communicate with them, it's essential to know how to read and use your nonverbal communication skills properly.

Reading nonverbal communication.

The first step to improve your non-verbal communication is to become skilled at reading other people's non-verbals. If you do not know how to read and interpret the body language of others, it will be incredibly hard to improve your own.

-**Start with the eyes:** What people do with their eyes can tell you lots of things. When you're talking to someone or are about to engage in communication with someone, try to pay attention to what they're doing with their eyes.

For instance, if you want to engage in conversation with someone, but that person is not making eye contact with you and is not aware that you're nearby, it would be wise to adjust your approach and make sure that you don't startle them. Once you start a conversation with someone, if you notice that they're not making eye contact with you (and are even evading your gaze) this might indicate several things: boredom, dishonesty or disinterest. This is especially easy to notice whenever someone is continually looking away and to the side.

If you instead notice that the person you're talking to is evading your eye contact, but they're looking down, this often indicates that they may be feeling uncomfortable, nervous or it also could be a signal of submissiveness. The size of their pupils can also tell you certain things. For instance, if you notice dilated pupils, this tends to indicate that you have the person's full attention, and in some cases, it might even mean that they're attracted to you. Pupils tend to dilate when we are making cognitive efforts, so if someone is paying attention to you, their pupils will unconsciously dilate.

Of course, it's not always easy to notice pupil dilation, but under the right conditions and some practice, you'll be able to spot this often.

Interestingly, even our blinking rate signals several things to those we talk to. For instance, if you are feeling anxious or stressed, your blinking rate will automatically increase. In some cases, an increased blinking rate may mean that you are dishonest and have something to hide. If rapid blinking is paired up with a constant touching of the face, then the likelihood of the person being dishonest dramatically increases.

Another way to tell if someone is lying is if they are looking upwards and to the right. On the other hand, looking upwards and to the left is associated with honesty and telling the truth. Whenever people are making things up and using their imagination they tend to look up and to the right, however, when they recall something true, they tend to look up and to the left to remember real events.

When we glance at something, we usually communicate desire. We can communicate that we desire both things and people with our eyes. For instance, if you're at a meeting that you don't want to be in and you're continually gazing at the door, you'll be signaling to others that you are eager to leave. If you glance at a person from afar, you communicate a desire to talk to them.

-The rest of the face: We can still learn lots of useful things by knowing how to read nonverbal cues in this area. The mouth can be particularly telling; for instance, the way someone smiles can say to you some critical information. Smiles can be genuine or fake. You can tell if someone is doing a real smile if they engage their whole face while doing it. If you've ever been told to "smile with your eyes" when someone is about to take a picture of you, it's because smiles tend to look fake when you only smile with the mouth. When you engage the eyes at the same time as the mouth, a smile feels much more genuine.

If you notice that someone throws around a genuine smile while you're interacting with them, then it means that they're probably enjoying your company. On the other hand, if you notice that they only smile with the mouth, chances are that they are only trying to look like they are enjoying your company, but in reality, they aren't. In a genuine smile, all the face is involved, particularly the eyes. If someone makes a very quick grimace right before they smile, then this means that they're merely hiding their dissatisfaction behind their smile. If you ever see someone "half smiling," then this typically means that they're sarcastic or they feel nervous or uneasy.

You can tell that someone is relaxed and having a good time or at least feels comfortable in the environment they're in if their lips look relaxed. A relaxed mouth is typically synonymous of a carefree attitude and positivity. On the other hand, if someone has their lips tightened, this might indicate discomfort, disapproval or distrust.

Also, if you ever see someone touching the lips or covering their mouth before speaking, this could mean that they're about to say something dishonest.

-Head movement: Even the pace that someone moves their head while speaking to you can tell you useful things, like their level of patience and interest. For instance, if someone is nodding slowly, they're probably very interested in what you're saying and want you to carry on. On the contrary, if someone is nodding very fast, this means that they are eager for you to finish the conversation or that they are feeling impatient for their turn to speak.

The way the head is tilted also tells us lots essential things. If you notice that someone is tilting their head to their side, then this can be a sign of interest. Tilting the head back can indicate that the person is suspicious of what you're saying or they're feeling unsure.

Because people tend to point their face towards those that they feel a connection with, if you're in a group and someone is talking, you can learn who they feel an affinity towards by noticing who they're pointing their face at. You can also tell who the ones in positions of power are by noticing how often the people in the group look at them. The same applies the other way: those that are seen as less important are looked at less frequently.

Something important to mention, however, is that head movement is more "conscious" than other types of nonverbal communication and it can easily be faked, so it's best to make a more thorough judgment by looking at what the rest of their body is doing.

-Reading space and distance: If you pay attention to how close someone stands or sits next to you, you'll learn a lot about how they view you. One of the most reliable indicators of comfort and rapport is proximity; the closer someone is to you voluntarily, the more likely it is that they feel comfortable in your presence.

On the other hand, if you notice that someone moves away from you when you get closer to them, this might indicate that they do not feel comfortable with you getting close to their personal space. A simple exercise to do is to go to a public area and notice the pairs or groups of people around you; can you tell what type of relationship they have by looking at the proximity between them?

However, it is essential to remember that cultural factors and upbringing can influence certain types of body language. For instance, certain cultures prefer there to be more distance in social interactions, so this is not always an accurate gauge of comfort and rapport.

-**Reading the arms:** Although the arms are one of the most manageable parts to control consciously, they can still tell you valuable information in many cases.

If you're interacting with someone and they have their arms crossed, this usually suggests defensiveness, and it can be an indicator of several things: the person might be feeling nervous and anxious or vulnerable. Crossed arms can also be a sign of skepticism or disagreement. In some instances, crossed arms may be accompanied by a real smile, which means that the person feels very comfortable and confident. If you ever notice someone placing their hands on their hips, they might be trying to look more dominant.

-**Reading the hands:** It is slightly more challenging to be conscious of your hands when you're engaged in a conversation. Because of this, they can give us important cues about how a person is feeling. Having the hands inside the pockets or the head is an easy way to tell that someone is dishonest, but it can also only mean nervousness.

If you're talking with someone and they're supporting their head with their hand and resting their elbow in a flat surface, then this might indicate that they're doing their best to focus and listen to what you're saying. On the other hand, if they're supporting their head with both elbows on the table, they might be feeling bored.

A useful clue to look out for when you're interacting with groups of people, such as in meetings, is to look at unconscious pointing. In meetings, it is common to point towards the persons you share an affinity with or feel close to.

Holding objects can also tell us useful information. For instance, if you notice that someone is keeping an object (such as a suitcase or a purse) between you and them, then they are probably using this as a barrier that is meant to help keep some distance.

-**Reading the feet:** Knowing how to read the feet can be incredibly valuable, because of how easy it is to leak information in this area of the body. When people are engaged in conversation with others, they often focus on controlling the areas of their bodies that tend to be most exposed, like the face and their body position. Because of this, the feet tend to be largely overlooked and can give us powerful information.

You can learn about which direction a person wants to go by only looking at the direction their feet are pointed at. If you see that someone is pointing their feet towards, you then this means that they are likely to have a favorable opinion about you. However, if you're talking with someone and notice that their feet are pointing towards a different direction, then this means that they are probably eager to leave and do something else.

The same applies to groups; if you want to learn who feels an affinity towards who, notice where people's are pointed.

You can also sometimes tell if someone genuinely likes you if their feet are pointed towards you and not towards another person while they're talking to you.

-**Mimicking:** Mimicking or mirroring can be an excellent indicator of rapport. If you're interacting with someone, you can quickly tell how much they care about having an affinity with you by noticing how much they are mirroring you. For instance, say that you've just met someone and you are talking for them for the first time at a café. You decide to place your elbow on the table and cross your legs. If you notice that the person does something similar after a few seconds, then this is a good sign that they're trying to form a connection with you.

Time to practice!

If you wish to practice and improve your nonverbal communication, the first thing to keep in mind is that you need to put your full focus on the present moment, or at least try to do so as much as possible. Doing this isn't as easy as it sounds, especially in the beginning, when you're struggling to keep a myriad of different things in check while you're talking with someone else.

When trying to improve your nonverbal communication, it is key to be fully present; if you're always thinking about what you're going to say next, or have other things in mind while in a conversation, you're almost guaranteed to miss important non verbal cues that tell you essential information about what others are really saying and meaning.

Because of the importance of being in the moment, knowing how to manage your stress and develop your emotional awareness can pay off in a big way.

Stress is one of your biggest enemies in this area, as it can put a massive dent in your ability to communicate effectively with others. Whenever we're stressed out and thinking about other things, the last thing we focus on is the person in front of us. Because of this, we're more likely to misinterpret signals or to send confusing messages ourselves. We may even relapse into our old unhealthy behaviors.

Remember that emotions tend to be deeply contagious. Have you ever felt uplifted after talking with someone that seemed to be happy? Or have you felt sad and blue after talking to someone who is depressed or is going through a difficult time? Because of this, remember to choose your interactions carefully.

If you are feeling upset and you have a difficult time managing your emotions, then you are likely to make others angry and make the situation worse. If you're feeling stressed, it's best to take some time to calm down before engaging with others, as it's best to start social interactions when you have a better emotional balance.

If you need to calm yourself down and reduce your stress levels, try to find something that consistently relaxes you and that you access quickly. For instance, some might feel more relaxed after they hear a piece of music they love, others get more relaxed through touch, (by squeezing a stress relief object for instance), while others need to meditate or take a few deep breaths to regain their balance. Because everyone is different, you need to experiment and learn what works best for you.

Modulating your voice tone

As you now know, your voice tone conveys a lot of valuable information. To make sure that your voice tone supports and even enhances the message you want to say, start to notice how it affects how others respond to you. You should also modulate it depending on the ideas you are trying to convey. For instance, imagine that you're trying to show a lot of interest in a particular topic when someone is talking. You could modulate your voice tone to sound more animated to reflect this.

If you tend not to pay attention to your voice tone, it might sometimes go in a direction that you don't want to. For instance, your voice pitch might get high when you're trying to get someone to like you or when you're feeling excited. It's not always a good idea to let your voice go high, because you might come across as needy to the other party. For others, a high pitch voice is not always pleasant to the ears.

You can practice depth by speaking mainly from your vocal cavity, throat and abdominal area. The further you go into the abdominal area, the deeper your voice gets. Remember that a lower voice tone helps you appear more commanding and authoritative. It also helps others feel more relaxed when we are speaking to them.

Most of us have a bad habit of speaking too quickly. Speaking fast might give the wrong impression: that we are overly excited or nervous for some reason. Whenever possible, try to keep in mind to sleep slowly, especially when you're trying to get your point across.

If you wish to add some weight to certain words and accentuate specific ideas, you can always vary the intensity of your voice. Emphasizing will help you grab the attention of the listener and add impact to your speech. Adding power by changing the tone in words or syllables can provide contrast and make certain words sound more attractive. Pauses can also help the listeners absorb and understand what you're saying.

They can also be used to emphasize specific phrases and add dramatic effect.

A lot of shy people struggle with voice volume. The best thing you can do is to try and match your listener's speech volume to make them feel more comfortable. Of course, this doesn't apply if the listener is shouting or speaking exceptionally softly.

Eye contact and anxiety

Maintaining proper eye contact is a crucial skill if you're trying to improve your communication. Whenever you fail to maintain eye contact, people will quickly think that you are evasive or disingenuine. On the other end of the spectrum, you can quickly go overboard with too much eye contact and appear intimidating or even confrontational.

So what's the trick for being well-calibrated with eye contact? Some experts recommend keeping eye contact for no longer than 4 to 5 seconds before breaking it for a moment before doing it again. If you're starting to feel awkward when maintaining eye contact, then there's a good chance that the person you're talking too is also feeling uncomfortable. Good eye contact should feel natural to you and others. When you choose to break eye contact and look away, don't look away too quickly, as this may make you appear nervous or not confident. Breaking your gaze to make a gesture is an even better idea than looking away since it seems more natural.

Whenever you're speaking to a group, you must try to maintain eye contact with every person of the group. If you choose to do eye contact with just a few or worse, just one individual, then people will think that you are only addressing those persons and not the group as a whole. Of course, you cannot always do this when speaking to huge groups of people, but try to make an effort to hold eye contact with as many as possible.

If eye contact feels currently feels weird to you, you might experience "eye contact anxiety," which is a feeling of discomfort about maintaining eye contact. Shy people or people that suffer from social anxiety tend to feel very uncomfortable about the mere idea of maintaining eye contact with others.

There are several effective strategies for overcoming this type of anxiety. Some people overcome this fear by building up their tolerance gradually. For instance, you can start by practicing eye contact with people that you feel very comfortable with, such as close friends or family. Once they feel at ease when maintaining eye contact with those people, you can then move on to holding eye contact with co-workers, colleagues, or people that aren't as close to you. After this is successfully achieved, then the next step is to try it on people that may give you more anxiety such as strangers or supervisors. If holding eye contact with close friends and family is too difficult, you could even try practicing on videos first. Try to make eye contact with characters on tv or internet videos before moving on to real people.

It may sound a bit silly, but it works!

Another strategy for beating eye contact anxiety is to start by looking at a spot slightly between someone's eyes or above them. If you find that even this is very difficult, you could try letting your eyes go slightly out of focus. Once you feel more comfortable when doing this you can start by looking directly at the person's eyes for short intervals.

Improving facial expressions

Using facial expressions the right way can sound like a minuscule change, but it is one that can have an enormous impact throughout your life. If you're someone that usually doesn't have a pleasant facial expression, then you'll probably have a hard time making new friends, starting a relationship, getting hired or making successful business deals.

On the other hand, knowing how to use facial expressions to support your words can make all the difference in these areas.

Making changes to our facial expressions can be tricky because we naturally don't tend to focus or pay attention to what our faces are doing while we interact with others. Being aware of our faces is the first step. Once you do this, it's much easier to make changes and have a more pleasant facial expression during social interactions.

The first thing to do is to look at yourself in the mirror and notice your standard, resting facial expression. Your resting facial expression is the default way that your face looks most of the time. Make an honest evaluation of your resting facial expression. If you were to encounter someone who shared the same expression, how comfortable would you feel when talking to him or her? If you are having trouble making a good judgment of yourself, you can always try asking friends and family for their honest opinion.

If you find that they aren't giving you any info (for instance, if they tell you that "it's just the way your face looks"), then you could try asking strangers their opinion about your true resting facial expression and which emotion you convey through it.

If you either notice that your resting facial expression is not pleasant or have others tell you, then it's time to make some changes. Some people have a very poor mind to muscle connection with their faces and are unable to control much of it at all. The first step is to try and wiggle your ears. As you do this, you might notice that you raise your eyebrows, open or squint your eyes and move your mouth a lot. Keep going until you are genuinely able to wiggle your ears. People that have good awareness over their facial muscles tend to be able to wiggle their ears. Once you can isolate the mouth area and eye area, try to make small adjustments until you finally find a resting face that looks more pleasant than the previous one. You can always use other people for feedback. Keep making adjustments until you find a resting facial expression that looks good to you and others.

Try to practice it as much as you can in front of the mirror so that it becomes ingrained in your mind and muscle memory. It will eventually become your default resting facial expression in no time.

If you tend to have nervous habits such as biting your nails or facial ticks, then these might undermine your efforts, and even if you manage to achieve a friendly-looking resting facial expression, people will think that you look uninterested, distracted or nervous. If you are having a difficult time noticing you're nervous habits, others can let you know whenever you do them, so that you're able to be aware of them and make adjustments if necessary.

Additional tips:

-Try relaxing your jaw and tongue. When you do this, the rest of your face will tend to follow suit and appear more relaxed.

-When talking with someone, try to raise your eyebrows a little, as this will help you seem more engaged and interested in what they have to say. If your eyebrows don't move at all, you may come across as too serious or uninterested.

-If you tend not to smile too much, then it's better to start as soon as possible. Smiling has a lot of benefits: it makes you look more attractive, it makes you look more trustworthy, and it even makes you feel good by lowering your stress levels. The simple act of smiling has been shown to slow our heart rate and release endorphins. It's incredible how moving a few muscles in our face can cause such a massive impact on our mood and how others perceive us.

Improving your posture

Having good posture is like having a solid frame that holds the rest of our nonverbal communication together.

It's essential to practice our posture both sitting or standing. How can you tell when you're having good posture? Basically when you're in a position that causes the least amount of strain on your body, especially on the muscles, bones, and ligaments.

If sitting down, your back should be straight and your butt should be against the back of the chair. Your feet should be flat on the floor, and the knees bent at an angle that causes no strain.

If you're standing up, imagine that you could draw an imaginary line that goes from your earlobes, then goes through your shoulders, hip area, knees and finally the midpoint of your ankle. Good posture is essential not only to appear more confident when talking to others but also to keep your joints and bones healthy.

In both sitting and standing up, the shoulders should always be relaxed.

If other people notice that your shoulders are up, they will think that you are feeling anxious or tense, which will usually put them on edge too.

Keeping good posture will also help you breathe better, which in turn will help you relax.

Whenever you're about to deal a challenging situation where you typically feel anxious or insecure, a couple of minutes of practicing "power posing" (standing tall and holding your arms towards the ceiling or standing tall with your hands on your hips) will immediately increase your confidence. Studies have found that power posing makes our bodies release more testosterone and reduce stress levels at the same time.

The best way to practice your posture is to look at yourself in the mirror and then make slight adjustments so that you see and feel what proper alignment should look.

If you're finding it very difficult to keep a good posture at all times, then you could try using reminders such as leaving notes in your room, house or car or wearing a bracelet.

Gestures

A lot of people wonder about what to do with their arms and legs when they're talking to others, especially if they're addressing a group.

As you know, when we use gestures the right way, they help enhance our message and make us appear as more confident and relaxed. On the other hand, incorrect use of gestures will confuse others and diminish the strength of our words.

Making big gestures can make you appear more confident, but it can be easy to go overboard with them.

An easy rule of thumb to remember is to avoid gesturing above your shoulders.

Even the position of our hands tells a lot of information to others. For instance, having "open hands" often signals honesty. Exposing our palms makes others feel reassured that we are not trying to hide something. Putting our hands inside our pockets sends the opposite message.

If you're trying to make a request, turning the palms up means that we're asking for a favor, but If we do the same with our palms up, then we might come across as bossy or demanding.

Saying something while holding our hands close to our hearts can make others think that we are genuine and sincere.

Your hands should be relaxed and by your sides so that you can quickly bring them up whenever you want to gesture. Remember to rest them down once you're done gesturing so that you come across as relaxed and positive.

Certain gestures can be distracting or hinder the image you're trying to convey. Some examples of these are:

-Placing the hands on your hips (makes you seem condescending or overbearing).

-Crossing your arms (signals disagreement or defensiveness).

-Hands inside the pockets (this may signal nervousness or that you're trying to hide something).

Some gestures can help communicate certain things.

For instance, having a hand raised acts as a stop sign. Thumbs up and thumbs down may signal agreement or disagreement. You can use your hands to show a specific shape.

You can also display certain emotions with gesturing, for example, clenching your fist signals anger and clasping your hands together signals pleading. Placing your hand over your heart can signal that you're feeling empathy for someone.

It's important to remember that cultures highly influence gestures. What a particular gesture means in one culture might have an entirely different meaning in another.

Fidgeting should always be stopped since it sends a visible message that you lack confidence and are feeling nervous.

Employers mention that they've rejected many candidates to a job position because of their excessive fidgeting. Fidgeting in this scenario could mean a lack of confidence and preparation.

Fidgeting could be anything from playing too much with your hair or fingers to biting your nails or shaking your foot. When we do these actions, the reason usually is because we are looking for a way to release some anxiety. When we fidget, we draw attention away from the message we're trying to convey and end up distracting people.

If you're a severe fidgeter, other people perhaps have mentioned this to you. If not, try to pay attention to what you do with your hands and feet the next time you're talking to someone; this can be especially useful if you're talking to someone you don't know very well since we tend to feel less reassured and thus may fidgeting more.

When this happens try to pay attention to how you fidgeting and what exactly acts as a trigger to those behaviors. Then try to think about other things to do with your hands and feet to replace the nervous body language.

Key points to remember

-Keep in mind that what comes out of your mouth and what you do with your non-verbal cues should be as harmonious with each other as possible. Avoid having a mismatch between these two.

-Avoid drawing a conclusion based on a single cue and try to look at a group of signals instead to make a better judgment.

-If you are not sure about what you're going to say, this will probably show in your body language, and people interacting with you will quickly grow confused or bored.

-Eye contact is critical, but you should also avoid staring at other people's eyes for too long, as it may place unwanted pressure and make them feel uncomfortable. Remember to break eye contact briefly from time to time to prevent this from happening.

-If you're feeling stressed or anxious during a conversation or public speaking, remember that it will eventually show in your non-verbals if you don't do something about it. An easy fix that helps in most cases is to slow down your talking pace and start taking deep breaths until you feel more at ease.

-If you interact with people from a different culture, it would be wise to do a bit of research to better learn about which gestures and non-verbal actions are okay and which aren't.

-Self-coaching can be extremely powerful. In my case, it was a great tool that helped me dramatically improve my nonverbal communication. To do this, you will need to record yourself while interacting with others. You can do this by placing a camera nearby and recording yourself while talking in the mirror. It is best if you have a target to shoot for, a role model that you think that has excellent non-verbal communication. It can be a celebrity, a public speaker, a politician or even a fictional character from a movie. Anyone that you admire or think that has good body language will work. Once you have something recorded, analyze what you're doing with your whole body and compare it to the role model you've chosen. If you're not happy with what you see, make some notes that will help remind you the things that you should be focusing on the next time. Continuously repeat this until you are satisfied with the results.

You can also ask a friend to record you while speaking to others. The same advice applies: analyze your nonverbals, make notes and always tweak what you see until you are satisfied with what you see.

CHAPTER 6: BUILDING EMOTIONAL INTELLIGENCE

Emotional awareness

You might be wondering why there's a section about emotional intelligence in this guide. There is a very simple answer to this: for us to send congruent and calibrated nonverbal cues, we must become aware of our emotions and how they affect our behavior.

In simple words, emotional intelligence is the ability to be aware of our emotions, how they affect us, and how they affect those that are around us.

Emotional intelligence also helps us understand better how others feel so that we can manage our relationships and interactions more efficiently.

Throughout your life, you've probably met some people that seem to be excellent listeners. No matter to whom they are talking about or the situation they might be in, but they always seem to have something great to say. And they also have a well-calibrated way of saying things in order not to hurt other's feelings. We tend to view these people as caring or considerate, and we often leave a conversation with them feeling uplifted.

Also, you might know a few people who seem to be in complete control at managing their emotions. Rarely do you see them stressed, angry, or upset. Whenever they are faced with a problem, they calmly try to find a solution to it. Because of this, they tend to be great decision-makers, and people tend to trust their intuition and choices a lot.

What do these two types of people have in common? They have a high level of Emotional Intelligence. They know themselves exceptionally well and can quickly sense other's emotional needs. They are also able to take criticism exceptionally well, and they know how to use it to improve their performance or skills.

Emotional intelligence has become more and more accepted as an essential part of our success in life, alongside technical ability and knowledge, and many organizations are starting to pay attention to this quality when they're hiring and promoting.

Having good emotional awareness also means that we too can recognize the emotions of others, especially their genuine feelings that may sometimes hide below the surface.

Most of us have the ability to develop and fine-tune our emotional intelligence.

Some are fortunate enough to have lived through the right conditions that made a high degree of emotional intelligence second nature to them.

Here are a few highly effective ways to develop our emotional intelligence:

-Learning how to reduce our negative emotions. Controlling and reducing our negative emotions is one of the Emotional Intelligence. Being able to properly manage our negative emotions so that they do not influence our judgment and decisions is critical.

If you've ever dealt with a difficult person or situation and your emotional intelligence isn't yet developed, you might jump to negative conclusions very fast. When in such situations, try to instead think about different angles to approach the issue before you react. For instance, imagine that you are going out on a date with someone, but they cancel at the last minute.

Instead of getting upset and thinking that it's because you're boring/uninteresting/not good looking enough, consider the possibility that they've been busy or have had an important event coming up that they cannot miss. The critical thing here is to avoid taking other people's behaviors personally. This way you can take their reactions with better judgment. It will also help prevent misunderstandings from happening.

A lot of people fear rejection and go through life, trying to avoid its sting. Being rejected, whether it is from a potential employer or a romantic interest can be devastating to those that don't know how to manage their emotions or have a fragile self-image.

Unfortunately, there is no easy way around getting over rejection: the best thing you can is to desensitize yourself to it. For example, if you fear being rejected by a member of the opposite sex, the only way to stop it from affecting you so much is to get rejected over and over again until it stops bothering you.

Easier said than done, right? In these situations, the gradual exposure exercise from before can help significantly.

Another option that can help you manage the sting of rejection is to have multiple options. For instance, say that you are applying for a job. If you get rejected or never get called back, you will probably feel hurt or incompetent to a degree. Instead, you could apply to several different job positions at once, and if one of them doesn't work out, there's still chance that one of the others will. You can apply the same principle to other areas of your life where you feel a fear of rejection.

-Building self-awareness. Science has demonstrated how our upbringing has a profound influence on our emotional experience. Our abilities to manage our emotions, such as anger, guilt, fear, pride, and happiness, are all heavily influenced by our early experiences in life.

If your guardians and caretakers placed a great deal of importance on your emotions, then it is likely that your self-awareness was developed to a degree where you feel like your emotions are valuable tools to navigate the world. On the other hand, if your upbringing was confusing, and you had emotional experiences as an infant or child that were painful, then you've likely distanced yourself from your emotions at some point.

Being able to be in tune with your emotions is key to understanding how the way you feel influences your actions and thinking. You could start by becoming more "emotionally literate." What I mean by this is to be able to name the emotions you feel so that you can know what's going on in your body. Some emotions tend to be very similar to each other, for instance, sadness and grief.

Because emotions can sometimes feel like powerful waves that take control over our body, it can be incredibly useful to be able to name our emotions; there's evidence that being able to name and identify our emotions can lessen their intensity. What we can recognize or identify is no longer a mystery. This ability can be especially useful if you distance yourself from the experience by using the third person voice. For instance, if your name was John, next time you feel angry you could say "John is angry." Or if you're feeling resentful, say, "John is resentful." This is much better than saying to yourself "I'm angry" or "I'm feeling resentful" because you immediately distance yourself from the negative emotion. By doing this technique, you will notice that you'll feel calmer and in control of the situation.

Another useful tip related to the above is to let your negative emotions be. Most of us have been taught to try to combat our negative emotions, so we tend to try to fight them as soon as possible. Instead of doing this, try to "observe them" and let them be.

Take a few deep breaths after you say something like "John is feeling frustrated." After saying this, try to identify if you can tell what exactly triggered the emotion. This simple exercise will help you recognize when you're heading down a path that won't do you any good.

You could even start to pay attention to how each emotion affects your body. There's evidence that different emotions have a different effect on our physical bodies. For instance, for some people, feeling anxious might make their palms feel sweaty, or their hearts pound faster. For others, feeling sad or depressed might decrease sensitivity in certain limbs. Whenever you start feeling an emotion, identify what exactly it is that they activate inside your body.

It is best to remember that all emotions, even bad ones, give us essential information that we can use. They all exist to help us in some way.

When we feel fearful or angry, we must ask ourselves what exactly is causing us to feel that way so that we can go for a specific course of action the next time we are facing a similar situation.

-Practice empathy. An essential part of being an excellent communicator is to be able to put yourself in the shoes of others, even if just for a brief moment. To be empathic means that you can recognize emotions in others and that you can understand their situation and reality.

Empathic people can go beyond only caring about their concerns and needs. Once you start seeing things in a variety of different perspectives, you'll notice that there's a lot to appreciate in this world.

The first step to practice empathy effectively is to put aside your viewpoint for a moment and try to see things from another person's perspective.

This can be especially helpful whenever you're discussing something with others. You might think that the person you are interacting with is being unreasonable or rude, but they are probably acting that way as a response to the situation they're facing.

Once you start seeing why people believe what they believe or why they are reacting in a certain way, you should acknowledge their perspective. Note that this doesn't mean that you should always agree with them. Acknowledging and agreeing are two separate things. Acknowledging that people have different opinions to your own and that they may have an important reason to hold those views will help you adopt an empathic stance.

The next step should be to examine the way you're reacting. Whenever you're interacting with others, are you only interested in winning or being right? If that's the case, your priority should shift to find a solution or make it a win-win situation. If you're close-minded, there won't be enough room to practice empathy.

Make sure that you are listening to the message that the person is trying to say. Use every resource available to make sure that you really understand their message. Focus on their tone, notice what they're doing with their body language and connect with your gut feeling and try to sense if they're genuine or not.

In some cases, you might need to tell the person to explain their position or to ask them what they would like to do. You won't always be able to figure out their point of view. There is no shame in not being able to figure it out on your own.

In terms of people skills, using an empathic approach is key to building strong relationships and becoming more influential, if that's what you seek. By practicing all of these things when you interact with people, you'll start to appear as someone that is genuinely caring and approachable and as a result, people won't be scared to open up and want to connect with you at a deep level.

Quick tips:

-Notice the way you react when you interact with others. Do you usually rush to make a judgment before you try to put yourself in the shoes of others or before you pay attention to all the facts? Be honest about the way you interact with people and the way you think about them. Putting yourself in their place will help you become more open and accepting of their points of view.

-If you hurt someone or do something wrong, don't avoid taking responsibility for your actions. People tend to be more willing to forgive if you honestly try to make up for your mistakes.

-Figure out if you're an attention addict. Being humble can be an excellent attribute, and practicing humility doesn't necessarily mean that you're timid or lacking in self-confidence. Whenever you practice humility you can allow others to shine and put focus on them.

-Everyone faces challenging situations in their lives from time to time. It's how we react to these stressful situations that help us or hinder our chances for success. Anytime you find yourself in a difficult situation, try to find something that you learned about it. Asking yourself constructive questions to help you figure out what you were able to take away from the challenging event.

Emotional intelligence evolves and grows over time as long as we have the desire to improve it. Every interaction, challenge, and person that we encounter in our daily lives is an opportunity to test our emotional intelligence and make it better. In the end, a highly developed emotional intelligence will only do wonders for our lives as a whole.

CHAPTER 7: DEVELOPING CHARISMA

Charisma is one of those words that evoke different things to different people. And it's not difficult to see why: charisma can be tricky to define, and we see people with diverse personalities being labeled as charismatic all the time. For instance, what do Bill Clinton and Muhammad Ali have in common? At first glance, maybe not that much, but they're both considered to be very charismatic and influential people.

It's best to see charisma as a label that we use to describe several personality traits. The two most important of these traits are power and warmth.

Have you ever felt warm and fuzzy inside after talking to someone? You probably felt that way because the person you were interacting with made you feel that way. Whenever someone can make us feel that way over and over again, we subconsciously think of them as magnetic or charismatic

One of the most potent abilities that charismatic people have is that they can easily connect with others thanks to their natural appeal. Whenever they interact with others, they make connections at an emotional level. People that speak with charismatic individuals feel like they are firmly understood, which is why many charismatic leaders have been able to influence the actions of thousands and even millions of people.

No wonder why being charismatic is such a desirable trait. At the same time, it is also considered to be a very elusive trait.

Just like with most skills related to interacting with others, most people believe that you are born charismatic and that it's not possible to improve this trait. However, this couldn't be further from the truth. It's possible to study, learn and put into practice precisely the things that make people charismatic so that eventually we know how to make the same deep emotional connections with others and leave them feeling fuzzy and warm after interacting with them.

How to develop charisma

So this all sounds good, but how exactly do we develop charisma? Such an elusive and highly sought after trait is undoubtedly very hard to develop. In reality, developing charisma is not rocket science; you need to look at the things you do under a microscope, find out what is working and what isn't, and make adjustments until you achieve the desired result, which is becoming more charismatic in this case.

You may not always like what you see when you do this, but it's the only way to identify which of your behaviors are hindering and which are helping you in social interactions.

Step 1. Developing your presence.

Some traits influence our judgment when labeling someone as charismatic, but arguably the two most important of these are presence and confidence. So what exactly is presence? In summary, it's about showing others that they have your complete attention when you're interacting with them.

You've probably talked to someone recently that didn't seem to be paying you much attention. He or she was perhaps showing signs of disinterest by avoiding eye contact, positioning their body in such a way that made you feel like they wanted to leave soon or maybe they were checking their phone often.

Remember that to be perceived as charismatic; you must be selfless when trying to connect with others. Have you ever been in a conversation where you are anxiously waiting for your turn to speak or even worse, interrupting others? This is precisely the opposite of what you need to be doing if you wish to become more charismatic.

At first, this may sound counterintuitive. After all, isn't charisma about being perceived as impressive and out of the ordinary by other people? Well, perhaps the best well-kept secret about charisma is that it's all about making the other person feel good first and foremost. A genuinely charismatic individual can make the person they're talking to feel extraordinary and awesome, and they leave a conversation feeling better than they were before.

Of course, this can be quite tricky at first, because most of us are wired to want to talk about ourselves and sometimes even boast about our best qualities.

So what are we to do? To start, we need to give full attention to the other person when we're in a conversation. We need to be excellent listeners and pay attention to everything that comes out of their mouth. If necessary, you can use visualization techniques to help you. Imagine that you're reading the person's biography and learning something new about them as they talk. The worst thing you can do is to be continually thinking about what you would like to say once they stop talking. It might sound like a good idea, as you're thinking about the perfect response, but in the end, it takes you away from the present moment and shows that you're not truly listening to the other person.

Step 2. Developing presence and confidence.

As mentioned previously, the two most essential traits of truly charismatic individuals are presence and confidence. Confidence plays a big part in being perceived as charismatic, and it's probably the trickier of the two to develop.

A confident individual knows what he's good at with precision and what type of value they provide to others. They also know how to act in a way that conveys this to the people they're interacting with. Being seen as confident by others boils down to having the ability to feel comfortable enough in your skin.

So how do you do this? The answer is highly individual. We all have different things that contribute our sense of confidence and impact it either negatively or positively. For instance, you might have noticed that you feel better about yourself whenever you dress appropriately, or you exercise regularly. Or you might have noticed that whenever you speak to strangers, you feel better about yourself afterward. If that is the case, then you should do these things more often to cultivate a healthy sense of confidence.

On the other hand, certain habits may impact your sense of confidence negatively.

For instance, you might feel crappy after you eat fast food, whenever you forget to exercise several days in a row or when you dress sloppily. If you have identified which things make you feel this way, try to do your best to minimize these habits and put most of your focus on doing the ones that make you feel better in your skin.

Confident and passionate people tend to be driven by purpose and goals. People that tend to be perceived as hesitant or not confident typically have low self-esteem and have little belief in themselves and their capabilities. If this is your case, then try to set small goals on something that you've wanted to achieve but have had a hard time with in the past. For instance, you might have wanted to lose 30 pounds, but you only managed to lose 15. In your mind, you probably see this as a failure, which will hinder you the next time you try to attempt to do the same. You don't believe that you can lose 30 pounds, because after all, you've never been able to do so in the past and you have no personal references to help you.

If you try to place small goals instead of bigger ones, you'll taste the sense of achievement more often, which will significantly promote a healthy sense of self-worth. Using weight loss as an example, instead of setting a big goal such as losing 30 pounds, reward yourself every time you lose 3 or 4 pounds. Experiencing achievement often is one of the most powerful things you can do to improve your self-esteem and confidence.

Another powerful thing that you can do for your confidence and self-esteem is to have a "mission" in life and to be able to live it and embrace it fully. Influential and charismatic leaders such as Gandhi wouldn't be perceived the same if it weren't for their compelling vision and mission driving their actions.

Step 3. Be humble.

This goes back to being selfless.

Charismatic people are known to be enjoyable to be around with and not arrogant. Sure, you might be very skilled at X thing, but it's not necessary to spew out your accomplishments or wave your trophies at every opportunity you have.

So why is being humble an essential step to developing charisma? It's all about being perceived as approachable and warm. Using a recent example, U.S. President Barack Obama is seen as charismatic by a lot of people, and a significant part of this is his humble attitude. He knows how to downplay his abilities intelligently, and you never hear him boasting or bragging.

When you are humble instead of arrogant or obnoxious, people don't feel afraid to open themselves more to you, which creates a window of opportunity for deeper connections.

Coupled with a humble attitude is not being afraid of showing some vulnerability. These two traits go hand in hand. When someone strives to be seen as perfect all the times, they create a gap between them and the rest of the world. On the other hand, when someone appears to be flawed, we tend to be drawn to them naturally. This is all backed up by science and is commonly known as the Pratfall effect: whenever you admit to making a mistake, you immediately become more likable. There's evidence that shows that people can connect better with others that admit their flaws and errors vs. those that try to appear perfect most of the time.

A lot of people are afraid to show vulnerability to the outer world. They associate vulnerability to negative things such as weakness or naiveness. Some of us are taught from a young age not to show vulnerability, as it is crucial to be successful.

In reality, real vulnerability is not about winning or losing or showing signs of weakness in your armor to the world; it's about having enough courage to show up and be seen by others even when you have little control over the outcome of a situation. Showing vulnerability means that you can be your authentic self with another person. This is what paves the way for the feeling of genuine connection and understanding.

There are also several ways that we can show that you're unguarded to the world. Here are a few examples:

-You show vulnerability when you share your struggles with others so that people can identify with you with greater ease.

-You show vulnerability when you talk about the flaws that make you look more human.

-You show vulnerability whenever you make a mistake, and instead of trying to hide it and appear perfect, you admit your error and what happened.

Showing vulnerability is one of the most challenging things to do as you work towards becoming more charismatic, as most of us are afraid of being judged and criticized. However, if you observe some of the most influential and likable people, they aren’t afraid of opening up at all. Keep in mind that showing vulnerability isn't the same thing as complaining. Complaining is probably the number one charisma killer. Vulnerability is about showing others that your human and not perfect.

Do not dismiss vulnerability, as it can be a potent trigger of likability.

Step 4. Be authentic.

A charismatic person tends to live a genuine life, and their actions and behaviors reflect this. Charisma and dishonesty are opposites. Of course, there have been people through history that have managed to be labeled as charismatic while being highly deceiving, but they are exceptions to the rule. It is easier to develop charisma while leading a genuine life.

Charismatic people tend to be genuinely interested in the concerns of others. When they are talking to others, they have a legitimate interest in what the other person has to say, on their interests, experiences, and circumstances.

We all know someone that becomes a radically different person depending on the environment he or she is in.

For instance, a particular person is probably aggressive at the workplace, likable when he's with his friends, and insecure in his relationships. They might be talking to you, and suddenly, their voice tone, body language and choice of words almost instantaneously change whenever someone else enters the room.

We've all acted without authenticity at some point or another. Acting like ourselves in most situations can be something challenging to do, especially when we're in unfamiliar situations or are under pressure or scrutiny.

Acting without authenticity tends to be a typical response to the fear of rejection. We fear that our usual self isn't good enough, so we behave differently to avoid rejection.

If you've ever felt uneasy when interacting with someone but you're not exactly sure why, it's probably because that person is not acting with authenticity.

They may be hiding something or are acting in a certain way to get something from you. We tend to be repelled by these people, even if we cannot point to the reason why. On the other hand, people are naturally attracted to authenticity. When someone is authentic and honest, their verbal and non-verbal communication reflects their motives. Even their micro-expressions (extremely brief, involuntary facial expressions that tend to be in line with the emotions a person is experiencing) signal that the person is honest.

Now, as mentioned, acting authentically at all times is not an easy thing to do. You can start by observing your behavior when interacting with others. Pay attention to your words, body language and actions. Whenever you notice that they shift and you begin to feel as though you're in someone else's skin or you've stopped acting like yourself, take note. If you've noticed that you tend to change because of a particular trigger, pay attention to what exactly is making you uncomfortable, and attempt to do something to improve the situation if possible.

Whenever you're talking with others, besides listening attentively, you can also ask questions that you're sincerely interested in. Don't ask questions just for the sake of it and to prolong a conversation. When you develop a genuine interest in what others have to say, it will be easier to form connections and feel like you're acting from the point of authenticity.

Step 5. Mixing power with warmth.

Some people have defined charisma as being a combination of warmth and power. Let's start by discussing power, as it's one part of charisma that many people tend to have trouble understanding. Power doesn't necessarily mean that you have power or control over others, but that you can remain genuinely confident in most situations you go through. Social confidence is especially important. The more socially confident you feel, the more comfortable you will be able to act from authenticity and the easier it will be to attract others and make them feel connected to you.

So how can we become more socially confident? Think about the situations where you tend to feel at total ease? Why is it? I can assure you that when you feel very familiar and in control of a situation and your mind feels reassured that nothing wrong can go wrong, your whole body is relaxed. One of the best strategies to become more socially confident is to take more social risks. Practicing this will skyrocket our social confidence in a short period.

So, what exactly is confidence? Let's say that you're very skilled at public speaking. When you first started, however, you probably were very nervous, and your first attempts at it probably left you very anxious and stressed. However, after your 20th or 30th attempt, you probably felt much more at ease, and you might even have begun to enjoy the process. Each time you spoke in public, confidence in your abilities increased. Little by little, what was terrifying became familiar.

So how can we apply a similar concept to social confidence? Whenever you're in a social situation, you have a variety of options at your disposal. There are several things that you can say at any moment during the interaction. Let's say that you have lots of social anxiety. In that case, your social confidence will probably be shallow and even though you have the same amount of options as most other people when they're in the exact situation as you, most of those options will seem scary, and you won't even consider them. Imagine that you knew the perfect story to tell but you're afraid of what others might think. You have that option, but it seems risky.

You would then keep your mouth shut, and others will never hear your story. As you gain more social confidence, more and more options will seem less risky to a point where they don't cause you any anxiety or stress.

To increase your social confidence, unfortunately, there's no easy solution: you must go out into the world and face your insecurities. Make a list of all the things that make you most anxious in social situations, and which typically keep you from acting genuinely and confidently. You must do the exposure exercise explained previously. For instance, if you're afraid of talking to strangers, you must start by asking for the time, and then slowly build up the difficulty with each training session. Once you feel confident with this, you could ask for directions. Later try to prolong the conversation as much as possible. The final goal might be to try and make a new friend by talking to someone that is a total stranger.

The most crucial part is that you feel what social pressure feels. If you have social anxiety, you've probably lived most of your life avoiding social pressure like the plague. To become socially confident, you need to become very familiar with the feeling of social pressure. Once you expose yourself to social pressure continuously, it will start to feel familiar and will not be a big deal anymore.

Other exercises to feel social pressure are:

-Try getting an item for free at a store. Go to any store you want, pick up an item, and try to convince the cashier in a friendly way to let you have it for free. You can also do a similar thing at a restaurant with the waiter. By doing this exercise, you'll feel a lot of social pressure, and you'll soon become familiar with the feeling if you do it often enough. As you'll notice, nothing terrible will ever happen. The worst thing that could happen is that the cashier and waiter will say no. You could even get stuff for free this way!

-Speaking to yourself loudly. Do this preferably in a public space where you're sure you won't get in trouble. Other people must be around for you to feel social pressure. You start talking loudly to yourself. You can say anything you want, but make sure that people that are passing by can hear what you're saying. This might feel extremely uncomfortable at first because you might feel terrified that others might think you're crazy.

Again, you'll feel lots of social pressure this way, which will help you a lot to become familiar with it.

-Do crazy things in public. Most of us are afraid of being seen as awkward by others. To familiarize yourself with awkwardness and thus, reduce the amount of social pressure you feel, you can try to do crazy stuff in public. Of course, you should never do anything illegal or actions that might harm you. Some ideas to get you going: dance or sing in public. Imagine that you're an actor and try to act like a character from TV or a movie that you enjoy. Sit on a busy sidewalk for a few minutes.

-Asking out members of the opposite sex. This is one of the toughest things that you can do, so it's probably best reserved once you've practiced the other social pressure exercises for a while. You try to chat with a member of the opposite sex and then ask them out on a date.

Most people are terrified of feeling the sting of rejection, and this can be a downright terrifying experience for them. It is for this same reason that you'll feel lots of social pressure quickly, which will help you feel more and more familiar with it so that you develop a thick skin.

Now that we've covered social confidence, we should talk about another critical way that others perceive power: through our non –verbal communication. Influential people tend to have body language and general non-verbals that signal power. Think about a powerful national leader and how they act whenever they are interacting with others. Or think about a boss or a CEO and how they act when they are talking to their employees.

To have body language that signals power, you should first and foremost, claim some space with your body.

Don't be afraid to take up some space (of course, be mindful of others, as you never want to be disrespectful) by spreading out your arms and legs. Make sure that your chin is straight and your back is straight. Never slouch. The shoulders should be slightly back to show that you feel at total ease in the situation. Avoid fidgeting with your hands.

You might not feel like you're comfortable and in control of a situation, so you might need to "fake it until you make it" initially. With time, you'll notice that by merely practicing powerful body language, you'll start to feel more powerful and confident naturally. Research can back this up: it has been found that powerful body language will decrease the production of the stress hormone cortisol, and increase testosterone at the same time.

The other crucial element of charisma is warmth.

Warmth by itself tends not to do much in terms of social appeal, but if combined with social confidence, you'll be an unstoppable magnetic force.

Let's start by defining what it is. Unlike power, warmth is what makes others feel like you're very approachable. Think about your favorite charismatic celebrity. He or she probably is known for being very approachable or at least does seem like it. It can be easy to mix presence with warmth, but they are different attributes. Warm people can provide a feeling of comfort whenever they interact with others.

If you currently lack warmth, there are a few things you can do that will be helpful: first of all, you should strive to treat others, no matter which background they might have, as equals. This applies in most social situations. Have you ever had a boss or superior that treated others like they were below him? This significantly contributes to his image of being unapproachable. It's precisely the opposite of what we're looking for.

To be seen as a warm individual, you need to genuinely treat others as equals and strive to make them feel good or important. Whenever someone makes us feel good, we are inevitably attracted to them. If you become a constant source of such feelings, people will start to become more drawn to you, since you are always providing them with positive emotions that they can look forward to in your next encounter.

The trick with power and warmth is to find the right balance of each. Too much power with too little warmth is not a good recipe. People will see you as cocky, arrogant, or unapproachable. On the other hand, too much warmth without power or social confidence will make you seem likable but insecure or needy. You should always be developing and experimenting with each of these qualities to arrive at the right combination that fits your personality and traits.

Extra tips for developing charisma

Don't ever complain

Sometimes, complaining, especially after going through a stressful event, can feel nice. However, a negative conversation is something that charismatic people avoid like the plague. Because of this, it's best if you completely stay away from any form of negative communication. Don't talk badly about others, give positive feedback instead of criticism, and never complain.

Strive to keep your conversations positive. This can be tough when you're interacting with someone that is being negative, and his vibe seems like it wants to latch on to you no matter what. In these cases, do the same with your positive vibe and try to get some of it on them.

If your friends and family or people that you talk to regularly are often negative in their conversations, make sure that you try to steer the tone or topics to something more positive; by doing this, they will quickly realize that with you there are only positive conversations to be had. Over time, they might even start changing their conversations or topics to something more positive without your input.

After talking with someone and the conversation was kept positive all the way through, they will remember you in a good light, and will typically feel better than before they started interacting with you.

Charismatic facial expressions

What is the first thing that crosses your mind when you're talking with someone that seems to have very bland facial expressions?

You probably think that they seem boring or don't seem to be very interested in what you have to say. As mentioned previously, it's crucial that others feel like you are genuinely interested in them or what they have to say, so you should avoid having unengaging body language.

Let's start with the face. Using a variety of facial expressions will help you punctuate your words, and make certain parts of your speech sound even more exciting. The key to doing this is practice and calibration. You don't want to try using a wide range of facial expressions before you check yourself on either a mirror or a video recording. This is because what you think that looks charismatic or cool may come off as over the top, distracting or creepy to others. You could even recruit the help of a friend or someone you trust that could give you some constructive criticism about the way you're using your facial expressions.

Also, don't forget to smile more often. It may sound simple, but people tend to feel better when you smile at them.

Using touch the right way

It has been found that using gentle touch while you're talking to someone will make it easier to keep them engaged and interested in what you're saying. Charismatic people tend to be masters of social touch. They know that touching others gently to emphasize specific points will give them better control of their conversation and makes others feel more relaxed and at ease.

A few words of advice on this, though. In some cultures or certain social circles, it may not be acceptable to touch others in social situations, so adjust your touch depending on your environment.

In most cultures, however, it's perfectly acceptable to do a friendly touch on the arm or the shoulder while you're talking to someone.

In other cases, some people don't like to be touched or don't want to be touched in specific areas such as the arms. It's best to be discreet and use the feedback that the person is giving you. If you notice that the person seems uncomfortable every time you touch them, try to use a different approach instead.

Touching can also be easily overdone. Even if someone is okay with gentle touches during conversations, they can start to feel uncomfortable if it's done too much. As a result, even if you've initially created great rapport, most of your work will be undone.

In summary, gentle touching can be a powerful tool but should be used with sufficient social calibration for it to have the desired effect.

Give compliments

A simple way to show others that you appreciate them is by giving genuine compliments. We sometimes go through life without ever paying attention to the efforts of others. Some people work very hard to learn new things, be good at something or improve their appearance.

By being a good listener and an acute observer, you will easily be able to notice important details about others. If you pick up on these and give them a genuine compliment, you will be immediately stand out from the vast majority that never does notice.

Charismatic people are very skilled at spotting these key things whenever they're interacting with others, and freely compliment them so that the person's efforts are acknowledged.

It can be hard to believe just how much they pay attention to critical areas and compliment can impress people. Doing this will also significantly speed up the rapport process.

Women tend to be better at giving compliments than men. So if you're a man and you become good at it, you'll definitively stand out from the rest of the crowd in no time.

A word of caution: what you should never do is give false compliments or be disingenuous, as people will tend to pick up on your inauthenticity and instead of feeling better, will feel awkward and uncomfortable.

Remember people's names

Say that you're talking to a stranger and you learn their name.

At some points during your conversation, you decide to say their name. Saying the name of someone you've recently met is an excellent way of giving them a subtle compliment. If you don't know how to start complimenting people, by simply saying their name at times during your conversation, you'll be able to make them feel better while in your presence.

Saying someone's name while you're talking to them signals that you respect and appreciate them enough that you made sure to remember their name. It makes them feel special and more excited to be talking to you.

If you're trying this on strangers and are having a hard time hearing their names, you can introduce yourself first instead of waiting for them to do it first. Once you've introduced yourself, asking for their name sounds very natural.

Once you've heard someone's name, make a mental note to remember it. Drop their name now and again, as it will help cement it in your memory quicker.

Slowing down

Have you ever talked to someone that seems to be speaking at such high speeds that you get exhausted in less than five minutes of listening to them? Or it may make it hard to build rapport with someone if all you're trying to do is keeping up with the conversation.

If you already have the habit of talking too fast, it's time to do a bit of work. Patterns like these can be especially tricky to break. You might be doing great one day, but the next you have entirely forgotten about it, and before you notice, you're talking fast again. An excellent way to break this habit for good is to use reminders.

Place these in your phone, in pieces of paper at your desk, or even at your nightstand so that it's the first thing you read when you wake up. The idea is to be always reminding you to slow down to break the habit for good. Some say it takes 21 days to break a habit; others say it takes much more than that. Everyone is different, and you should experiment a bit until you can finally manage to slow your talking speed for several days in a row without the need for a reminder.

As with most topics discussed in this book, it's important to find the right balance. Talking too slowly will quickly bore or frustrate others. If people think that you're talking too slow, you might notice that they start finishing your sentences. As a result, you'll lose their respect, and it will be challenging to build rapport.

Try to speak at a similar pace that the other person is speaking. However, if you notice that they're talking too fast or too slow, try to adjust your speed slightly so that they can hopefully do the same.

Using clever pauses here and there will add a lot of heft to your words and will help you emphasize important points. Small pauses will work wonders to keep the other person engaged in the conversation.

The correct mindset

You might be doing great at improving your body language, at modulating your voice and at making others feel at ease with your touch, but you will never be genuinely charismatic if you're approaching it all with the wrong mindset.

Just as you will need to work on your nonverbal communication and your social confidence, you need to spend some time developing the right mindset to be charismatic. Because of this, let’s take a look at some of the essential qualities and mindset that a charismatic individual needs to develop:

- Remaining optimistical: Great leaders such as Winston Churchill are known for their contagious optimism that was powerful enough to inspire and give hope to the masses. Being optimistical will help not only you but others to stay positive when times are tough. If people look up to you for inspiration and hope, they'll immediately feel a connection to you.

-Be passionate: Have you ever felt good after hearing a speech from a passionate individual. You may have had a teacher at school that seemed to have a significant amount of love towards his work, and found his passion highly contagious, even if you weren't a big fan of his or her subject.

-Nurture your curiosity: Just as a child is continuously curious about the world around him, a charismatic person feels very intrigued and interested in the lives of others. Nurturing your curiosity will help you ask excellent questions, and thus, you'll be able to learn exciting things about the persons you're talking to.

Asking great questions makes anyone feel appreciated.

-Don't be too predictable. People tend to feel attracted to what they aren't able to fully figure out. If you can think about some of the most charismatic people in history, you'll find out that most of them have a sense of unpredictability or mystery surrounding them. By not letting others figure you out completely, they will be naturally drawn to you, and you'll gain their admiration and interest with greater ease.

CHAPTER 8: THE ART OF NEGOTIATION

It's common for people to think that they're poor negotiators. In some cases, just thinking about negotiating can make some feel nervous or stressed. There could be many reasons for this: many of us believe that negotiating it an "all or nothing" event where one side has to lose for the other to win. In reality, this is incorrect. While it is true that when negotiating, the goal is to get what we want, some of the best deals involve terms and ideas from all parties.

Being a good negotiator is related to having excellent social skills. After all, we need to negotiate all the time, whether it is to get a new job or a raise, getting our friends or family members to help us with something essential or buying something locally or online.

In the end, negotiating is all about human interaction, and we should strive to make sure that we get everyone involved to the best result possible.

Preparing for the negotiation

Before we even start negotiating, it's important to think about what exactly we'd like to achieve from the process. Most people that are afraid of negotiating don't ever think about having a strategy. They put no thought into the person they're talking to, or have done any research to learn more about their situation so that they can approach the negotiation with an ideal angle.

Start by thinking about what would be an excellent deal for you — the best possible outcome. Then try to think about other fall-back positions that you would still be okay with. Think about as many scenarios as possible when doing this.

Something that can be extremely useful but is rarely done is to come up with a list of reasons why their proposal would benefit the other party. This will help shift your focus from trying to win to arriving at a position that will benefit everyone involved. You can even bring up the reasons when you're in the actual negotiation.

Be aware of the deal breakers

It's important to know what your deal breakers are with precision. Think about what would happen if there's no deal made. It's also a good idea to think about what the other party's walk away points would be and think about what will happen if they aren't able to make the deal. This is a useful exercise because it helps you better understand why they would or wouldn't be flexible. Not all negotiations are meant to end with a successful deal. It's wise to know what the deal-breakers are and realize that if that point is ever reached, it is fine to walk away.

It's also crucial to understand how you'll be able to get where you want to go. A lot of people come up with their goals for the negotiation but don't think about the process itself. Ask yourself how you will be able to get the deal done. What are the steps you need to take to get there?

The negotiation

Ideally, everyone involved should identify their goals at the beginning of the negotiation. This can be extremely helpful to understand where everyone stands. At this point, each party can say their fall back proposals and counteroffers.

If you're negotiating in person, you can gauge how the person received your proposal by reading their body language.

For instance, if you notice that they're giving you eye contact and don't have their arms folded, that's a positive sign that they're opening up to what you're saying. On the other hand, if they are avoiding your eye contact and they are folding their arms or subtly shaking their heads, then you might want to try a different approach.

If you are very good at reading body language, then negotiating in person might be the best option. However, this won't always be possible and you will find yourself negotiating over the phone or e-mail/text messages occasionally. If that's the case, try to use all the information available to you. If you're speaking over the phone, try to interpret the other party's voice tone. Their pauses can also tell you if they are thinking about the offer or if they're hesitant. If you notice that their voice tone sounds eager or they are swift to respond, then you can tell that they are considering what you're offering. If you're negotiating over text, then you can check for words or phrases that may indicate that they are open to your offer. Some examples of this might be words such as "possibly", "could" or "perhaps.

If the other party says something similar to "looking forward to your response," then you can be quite sure that they're enthusiastic and that getting to an agreement will be easier than expected.

If you're having trouble getting to an agreement, then there are a few things you can try. Whenever you want your point of view acknowledged by someone, it's crucial to acknowledge theirs first. It's a common mistake to think that to get to the outcome you want, you will have to do most of the talking. Instead, you should be listening a lot and asking several questions. Being a good listener means trying to understand what a person's situation is. Find out what their constraints are and what they're up against. This will help put you in the right frame that will increase the chances of getting the results you seek. Making sure that the other party notices that you acknowledge their point of view will make them much more open to hearing your point of view afterward.

Plan B

If you've done your preparations, then you'll know where to go in case things don't work out. If you're not able to find an agreement, try to leave the door open for negotiations in the future. If possible, schedule another meeting for another time. Try to make it sound like you honestly think that a deal can be worked out and that you're willing to put in the work to get there.

A simple exercise you can do in between negotiations is to try and review the initial meeting. Try to think if there was anything that revealed a weakness in the opposing party. Also, think about the factors that might influence whether the deal is made or not. Thinking about these factors can help give you an advantage during the next meeting.

Dealing with backlash

Backlash occurs when one party tries to over-negotiate and the result isn't what they expected. If people feel that you're trying to take advantage of them, they'll feel angry or resentful. Even if you manage to make a deal, you'll damage your relationship, and they will carry that resentment with them the next time you try to negotiate with them. Feeling like you've been taken advantage of is also something that can happen to you, so it's essential to know how to avoid it.

To avoid backlash, make sure that you only accept after giving enough thought to the situation. Rushing into a decision too quickly will often lead to negative emotions such as regret and resentment.

Try to tone down your excitement when things are working to your favor.

If you look overly excited when negotiating, the other party might feel as though they are giving away too much and will quickly feel resentful or reconsider the offer.

If you need to give bad news during a negotiation, do it all at once. On the other hand, don't be quick to deliver good news. Do it in stages.

Remember to be flexible at all times. When you give someone choices, they will feel involved in their decisions instead of feeling forced into doing something. Always try to have several options. Even if you can't be flexible on certain things, such as the price or the time, you can probably think about terms or something else that will help them feel more involved in the process.

In the end, we should always strive to see the other party in a negotiation as our partner in achieving the best outcome for everyone involved.

Applying the previously mentioned strategies will help you feel more at ease before starting negotiating because you'll realize that there's no need for anyone to come out as a loser and that you already have the necessary skills to be a good negotiator.

CHAPTER 9: DIFFICULT CONVERSATIONS AND COMMON DIALOGUE OBSTACLES

In our lives, we will inevitably have to face countess crucial, challenging, or fierce conversations that are both inevitable and important. It could be anything from delivering unpleasant news, to discussing a touchy subject or asking someone to change something that has gone wrong or isn't working. You could have these conversations with pretty much anyone in your daily life – from your partner to family members, friends, coworkers, and bosses.

If we don't feel very confident about handling these tough situations, then we will probably put them off as long as we can. Think about all the times you've needed to talk to someone because of an important reason, but you don't.

Maybe you've been in a similar situation in the past, and it didn't go well. Or perhaps your main fear is that talking will only make matters worse. In any case, you feel stuck in this uncomfortable situation and would like to find a way out. The bad thing about these conversations is that just thinking about them will give us negative mental baggage and will end up distracting and affecting us from doing other important things that need our attention.

What to do before dealing with a challenging conversation

The first step is to ask yourself a few questions before starting a difficult conversation.

-What is your objective for having this conversation? Identify what you'd like to accomplish (if anything) or picture the ideal outcome. A key thing to watch for is hidden purposes.

For instance, you might think that you have justifiable goals that sound honorable on paper (such as educating a child or teaching something to a co-worker), but then you use condescending language or are very critical with your words. Or you might want to help someone, but you end up punishing them. Some goals are genuinely justifiable though. Make sure that the conversation is only worth it if there's something positive to get out of it.

-Are you making any assumptions about the person or persons that you will have to talk to? Maybe you're making a few false assumptions that are in no way justified: for instance, imagine that you've spoken with the same person in the past, and you ended up feeling belittled or offended. The reality is that impact not always equals intent. Try to be cautious and identify the person's real intention.

-Identify what triggers you. Think about the previous times you've had difficult conversations and try to determine if there are any particular buttons of yours that tend to be easily pushed. Do you tend to be more emotional than what would be necessary for that situation?

-The next step is to identify is your attitude towards the situation is influencing your perception. For instance, if you think that something is going to be an awful experience, it's more likely that it will be. On the other hand, if you believe that even if it's going to be tough, there's something positive to get out of it in the end, then it's more likely for that to happen. Adjusting our attitudes can be extremely simple, but doing this can have powerful effects.

-Who are you going to be talking to? What do you think his or her thoughts are about the situation? Is this person aware of the problem, and if so, how do you think he or she perceives it?

What do you think this person will propose as a solution? Instead of looking at this person as your opponent, start thinking about him or her as a partner that will have to work with you to find a solution that benefits everyone.

-Finally, ask yourself how you or the other person have contributed to the problem.

Don't worry about pleasing everyone

People that tend to delay or avoid difficult conversations tend to be worried about how others perceive them, and specifically their likability. The desire to please others is natural for us human beings, but it's rarely essential. You should strive to be present in the conversation with an open mind and an honest desire for learning. If you approach the situation from a place of both curiosity and respect for you and the other party involved, things will be much simpler.

Pretend that you don't know much and try to learn as much as you can about the other party and their point of view. If necessary, you could even pretend that you're talking to someone from an imaginary place that you're not familiar with, and because of this, you need to find out what are their priorities there and how certain events can affect them.

If the other party were truly from say, another planet or species, then you'd probably be watching their every move and listening to their every word intently. Notice if you can find out what they want and if there seems to be something they are not saying.

Don't interrupt your conversation partner and let them talk until they are truly finished. The only exception is interrupting to acknowledge something they've said. Try not to take things personally. This is the phase where you have to try to learn as much as you can from your conversation partner.

Your turn to speak will come soon.

Making the other person feel heard and understood

Acknowledging your conversation partner helps them think that you've listened and understood what they're trying to say. Aim to understand their point so well that you could even make their argument for them. You can try actually doing it and explaining back to them what you think their point of view is. It will be much easier to get to an agreement if the other party sees that you realize where they stand.

Start acknowledging your negative behaviors. For instance, if the argument becomes heated, you may say something like, "I've noticed that I started getting defensive after hearing that your voice sounded condescending and aggressive. All I want is for us both to get to an agreement".

Doing this will help bring the conversation back to a point where emotions aren't influencing the flow as much.

Don't sweat it: remember that acknowledgment and agreement are two separate things. Acknowledging others' opinions doesn't mean that you have to go with their decision.

Your turn to speak

When you're sure that the other party has expressed most of their energy, it's then your turn to speak. If there's anything that you can see from your perspective that the other party may have missed, you can help clarify your stance without minimizing theirs. For instance, imagine that an employer has been telling you how you're often late, and from his perspective, it seems like you don't care at all about the company you work for.

– "I understand that you've concluded that I don't care about this company, especially since I've been late to work a few times this week. However, I can assure you that I do care about this company and my performance. I've been getting late to work due to some family-related circumstances, but that has been taken care of and shouldn't be an issue moving forward. Perhaps we can talk about how to address the fact that it seems that I don't care about the company".

Solving issues

You're then ready to start looking for solutions. Your best allies are asking questions and continued inquiry. Ask the other party what they think might work. Afterward, try to build on something that you like based on what they say. If at any point the conversation gets heated, go back to the inquiry phase. Asking the other party for their point of view usually makes them feel safe and encourages them to engage in the conversation.

If you've been successful in doing everything correctly so far, then finding solutions won't be difficult.

Tips:

-Try to be as direct as possible. Addressing challenging or uncomfortable situations head-on by getting straight to the point is the best approach one can take. Being respectful when engaged in a difficult conversation helps diffuse the heat and tension and often creates mutually rewarding outcomes.

-Remember to spend most of the time focusing on what the other party is saying. People that avoid conflict tend to spend lots of time going over their thoughts to feel better prepared. It's better to take the pressure off yourself. Remember that the most important thing to do in a difficult conversation is to listen, reflect, gather as much information as possible and ask some follow up questions.

-Never assume that the other party can see things from your point of view. In most cases, you will have to explain in great detail your thoughts about the matter.

-Always keep your purpose in mind so that you can quickly return to it when things get heated.

-If the other party attacks you verbally, instead of reacting similarly, try to help them recenter.

Conclusion

There is no denying that the world we live in is a social place and most of our time is spent as a member of various groups: family, friends or workplace.

For most people, becoming a good conversationalist and developing strong social skills will take a reasonable amount of time and effort. Depending on where you currently are, it might take you less than a year to a few years to feel completely confident and in control when talking with others. Personally, it probably took me a couple of years of consistent practice until I finally felt like I was a pretty good conversationalist and others started taking notice and complimented me on it.

No matter how much time it may take you, remember that getting this sorted out will bring massive benefits to your life. Nowadays, I truly feel like I'm a different person compared to where I was before. Connecting with others over a great conversation probably tops the list of the activities that I enjoy the most. The fear and anxiety that plagued me before having a conversation with someone new have now been replaced by a true sense of excitement. Every single interaction you have with someone can have the potential to change your life. Even if you feel uplifted after having a great conversation, you have improved your mood for the day, and it counts as a small success. I now wonder where each interaction will take me, and it feels me with joy to know that I'm now able to do things that I previously thought were exclusive to a lucky few.

Thank you, and good luck!

About the Author

Zac Cruz is a personal development author and musician who is on a mission to empower people to harness their infinite potential so they can pave the way to positive transformation in all areas of their lives. With first-hand experience of what intense shyness, bad habits, and lack of organization can do to one's overall confidence and quality of life, he ultimately took matters into his own hands and turned his life around. Going from timid to tenacious and from stagnant to flexible, he truly understands every challenge one faces along the way and has made it his lifelong purpose to help others step into their best versions.

CPSIA information can be obtained
at www.ICGtesting.com
Printed in the USA
LVHW081316310520
657006LV00028BA/2686

9 781646 940035